STONYGROUND

STONY GROUND

THE MAKING
OF A
CANADIAN GARDEN

DOUGLAS CHAMBERS

ALFRED A. KNOPF CANADA
1996

PUBLISHED BY ALFRED A. KNOPF CANADA

Copyright © 1996 by Douglas Chambers
All rights reserved under International and Pan American Copyright
Conventions. Published in Canada in 1996 by Alfred A. Knopf Canada,
Toronto. Distributed by Random House of Canada Limited, Toronto.

Canadian Cataloguing in Publication Data

Chambers, Douglas
Stonyground, The making of a Canadian garden

ISBN: 0-394-28154-3

1. Gardens - Ontario - Walkerton - Design.
2. Stonyground (Walkerton, Ont.) I. Title

SB473.C53 712'.6'0971321 C95-932877-7

First Edition

Jacket photographs by Norman Track and Vivian Gast
Inner photographs by Norman Track, Vivian Gast and Douglas Chambers
Plans by Eric Klaver
Author Photo by Nir Bareket
Jacket and book design by Jonathan Howells

Printed and bound in the United States of America

To my cousin Campbell Johnston
without whom it could not have been done

TABLE OF CONTENTS

LEGEND

A. Peter Day Memorial
B. Abbyss' Stone
C. 'Utile Dolce' *(Horace)*
D. Pope Monument
E. 'Pale Beneath the Blaze' *(Coleridge)*
F. 'Attende'
G. 'Ara Pacis'
H. Apollo
I. Pendulum
J. 'Dapes Inemptae' *(Virgil)*
K. 'Rust Roest'
L. 'Severall Mountings' *(Walton)*
M. Sundial 'reckon'd but with herbs'
N. Michael Wade Memorial

1. Potager
2. White Garden
3. Black Garden
4. Fountain
5. Great Garden
6. Barn Lawn
7. Cutting/Drying Bed
8. Tree Nursery
9. Rockery
10. Ha Ha
11. Terrace
12. Rose Bed
13. Compost Yard
14. Nursery
15. 'Gugliano'
16. Hedge-on-Sticks
17. 'Jekyll Border'
18. Rose Border
19. Carpark Border
20. Pumphouse
21. Arbour
22. Pergola
23. Shrubbery
24. Hill Garden

SCALE (in metres)

0   10   20   30   50

PREFACE

I sit in my study at Stonyground on a February morning. It is an old room papered in chinoiserie wallpaper in 1923 in an old house built in 1870. Originally this was the parlour — a room never used except for special occasions. A fretwork screen decorates the arch that joins what were once two rooms, and below it is the long harvest table on which I write. As the museum of the house, this parlour of my childhood was filled with memorabilia: a loon, now stuffed, that my grandmother had rescued from a ditch and nursed to tameness; my great-uncle Hugh's bayonet from the First World War, great-uncle Lorne's wind-up phonograph, with its brittle scratchy disks of Harry Lauder and John McCormack.

As I write, the sun shines in direct from the south over a landscape covered with snow and ice. After three days of ferocious storms, a respite, and one in which, even in this sub-zero weather, I can see the willows and poplars and alders already brushing up to green and yellow in the wet woods across the road: land once cleared, now long gone back to swamp. Things are beginning to move again on the roads. No one remains "storm-stayed" in the country for long; the determination, the need, to get on with things is too strong.

I think about the gardens and about the landscape as a whole, the 150 acres of it stretching away across sleeted fields to the tall woods to the north. This addiction to gardening is ineradicable once it gets hold of you. At this time of the year, it leads you to buy far too many seeds from the nurseries and to devise plans for summer that would employ a whole army of gardeners. I know this, but I do it nonetheless.

Where did it come from, this urge? For most of my life I had no garden, and yet I dreamed of this one, a lost garden of imagined memory to which I might one day find the key. The sources of Stonyground's inspiration are as invisible as the great underground river flowing beneath it that connects Lake Huron and Georgian Bay through unexplored caverns of prehistoric limestone. In his poem "Kubla Khan", Coleridge called the secret river of his inspiration "Alph": the letter "A", the beginning. But that beginning is also in the listening and the attending to what is already there, waiting to speak. And so much of that attending involves the escape from noise: literal noise, and

The house in winter looking across the rose border
and the long border

the babel of fashion, those great curses of our time. The God of the Old Testament asks for stillness; so does the muse of the garden.

No one who arrives in a revved-up Camaro or Trans-Am gets time in my garden, and if they come with the sort of super-hyped car stereo that can be heard a quarter of a mile away, their stay is even briefer. I spent (and spend) a lot of my time planting trees to shut out that sort of gratuitous clamour, and I think fondly of that French chain of hotels, the "hôtels du silence" where no radios or TVs are permitted, and cars have to be parked five hundred feet away.

"Why do you not have a cell phone with you when you're working?" ask people who cannot imagine ever being disconnected from an electronic nanny. Nor do they understand that one of the great joys of gardening is to escape from the cyber-gabble that eats up most of our lives: voice-mail, E-mail, all of it the chain-mail of an electronic culture that prevents us from really seeing and hearing. Gardens cannot be made to the sound of music either — any kind of music. They require concentration and, in the process, the total gift of the self to what is there to be discovered.

A true garden is never apart from its landscape. It arises from it like Eve from Adam's rib; it makes love to the fields in the language of botany. What I am doing in the gardens of Stonyground speaks back to the landscape what I have learned from it. Somewhere there is my father naming the spring wild flowers on walks in the woods, an uncle's mysterious cabinet of wild seeds, my grandmother in her large straw hat weeding among the flowers in her border, the last white pine preserved by a great-uncle from a speculating lumberman.

And over and around these things are stories, as indelibly a part of the place as the sweet rocket and money plant (or "silver dollar", as it's called here) that still run riot in the neglected corners in springtime. These are the stories that my great-aunts told about this place, their place, and about the family history that preceded it: stories of resistance and of making a new life. Told over and over again, though never exactly the same, they are as much a part of the fabric of this place as the maples planted by my great-grandmother that overshadow the house.

But I have also been taught how to appreciate these stories and to decode their real meanings by some of the great gardeners and garden writers of the past. The history of this garden is part of the history of gardens generally, and I needed to learn that language in order to understand the meanings of my garden. And that is why Stonyground is also a sort of history of the history of gardens, a collection of references and symbols that celebrates how this knowledge has been discovered and passed down.

One of these horticultural forbears, from whom I learned to "read" my own garden, was the eminent twentieth-century English gardener Gertrude Jekyll. She found the inspiration for her garden borders in the cottage gardens of Surrey: gardens that agricultural labourers had made from the flowers in the lanes and hedgerows where they worked.

And so she took the quiet beauties of these ordinary lyric places and gave them epic settings.

In a culture that prized the garish horrors of marigolds in carpet-bed plantings, what she did was as startling to her contemporaries as it is to North American tourists now. For here, in the famous gardens of Sissinghurst and Great Dixter and Hidcote that are indebted to her influence, are the ordinary weeds of our countryside: goldenrod and Joe-Pye weed and black-eyed Susan. Indeed, these and the cardinal flower and blue lobelia and viper's bugloss (that the locals here call "blue devil") were the very plants collected in the 1690s by the great horticultural pioneer Mary Capel Somerset, Duchess of Beaufort, and propagated in her gardens at Badminton.

Dazzled by the polyester vulgarity of shocking-pink impatiens and red salvia and "fire-chief" petunias, we miss the simple elegance of these roadside beauties. "Now," said a scandalized local visitor to Stonyground, confronting some Queen Anne's lace in the rose bed, "if that were in my garden, I'd have had it out." Behind me, in my memory, I could hear the ghostly cackle of my great-Aunt Ella laughing about the gentrified affectations of her city sister when she visited here. "All week she worked, pulling up those pink flowers in the border. 'Now you get the rest of that sweet rocket out of there,' she said to me." Aunt Ella laughs. "It's coming up there again now as thick as hairs on a dog's back." These stories are also the garden's sources, the voices of its muse.

But its source was in Eden too, Milton's Eden, the Eden of *Paradise Lost*. Where had Milton's ideas for a paradisal garden come from? I had wondered, early in the 1970s, when I began to work on a book on that subject. The flowery arbours and wooded alleys looked Italian, but the cattle and tedded grass were out of the English agriculture of the seventeenth century. Milton's Adam and Eve live in paradise, but they work in a garden that is also a farm. And out of such a vision came the English landscape garden. Why could I not reimagine such a thing here? And so it began.

When I think back now on how the gardens here came to be made, I am often amazed (and exhausted) by the thought of what has been achieved. Not that I have done it all myself . . . or could have done. One of the greatest pleasures is the great army of people, local and even international, who have participated in making the project. Their involvement has been more than simply at the level of labour. For when I try now to think how some things here came about, I realize that there is an inextricable web of suggestion and modification in which what *I* thought played only a part: a controlling part ultimately, yes, but a part nevertheless. And inevitably I wonder whether this has not been so with many of the great English gardens too: as much the Sissinghursts and the Hidcotes in the twentieth century as the Stowes and the Stourheads in the eighteenth.

When I began, I thought despairingly of the army of craftsmen that these British gardens seemed to have at their

The agricultural landscape in midsummer looking
back to the barn and the house

doorsteps: gardeners, woodworkers, stone-carvers, artisans of all kinds. Where would I ever find such people in Ontario, in Bruce County? At Stowe, George Clarke (its historian) had even found a hot-air balloon to take him up in the drought of 1976. And so he was able to prove that his theories of the work of the early garden designers there could still be seen beneath the dried lawns and burnt grasses of that summer.

But my fears were unfounded. Ten years after the inception of Stonyground, I have a farmer (my cousin Campbell Johnston) who has made me an extensive series of gardens with a bucket tractor. I also have a gardener (Tim Maycock) who is a glass-blower, metalworker, and cabinet-maker — a man who can make a garden seat from a hayloader wheel or a gate from a set of harrows, or transform a walnut tree into an armoire. Almost from the beginning I have also had a stone-carver (Tobey Soper) who can deal with everything from native granite to imported limestone, and manage a Latin inscription or an artist's signature. Only recently, moreover, a local couple (Paul and B.J. Guest) has turned up with a hot-air balloon — and a photograph taken from it that shows all the erratic geometries of my garden that are invisible on the ground.

Why have I written this book? Partly because I feel somewhat evangelical about what I have been (and am) doing: the ordinariness of it. It is not something that requires a landscape-architecture firm, nor need one own a department store to fund it. More to the point, it's important that the increasing number of urban people who are buying farms recognize that the agricultural cycle is beautiful and invigorating. Agriculture, the landscape that surrounds us, is the rest of the story of the garden: a story we here in Ontario have only begun to think about writing.

In his Reith lectures for the BBC, Sir Frank Fraser Darling wrote:

> *Most people will never know true wilderness although its existence will not be a matter of indifference to them. The near landscape is valuable and lovable because of its nearness, not something to be disregarded and shrugged off; it is where children are reared and what they take away in their minds to their long future. What ground can be more hallowed?* *

I would like to think that some of that love for that near landscape (and the mania) comes through in my writing. Has any culture lasted long without a love of place, a love that encompasses its stories, its mythologies, the mystery of its ecology? Stonyground is not the only place of its kind, by any means, but it is the place I know, know now at my frayed fingers' ends. It is the place to which my ruminating mind returns in any idle moment: doodles, speculations, pipe-dreams.

* *Wilderness and Plenty* (LONDON: BBC, 1970).

A friend calls up to talk about a garden temple: a long-put-off project. Could that temple be made with a vast sewer tile: a giant joke on all those little eighteenth-century outhouses called "Temples to Cloacina", the goddess of the sewers? What about the footings, the cost of the concrete, the source of the dome? "Yes, yes, send me some details, some suppliers." The storm goes on howling. I start a list of first things, March things: the shelterbelt spruces to be thinned and moved; the remaining branches from the felled maples near the house to be burned; the site of the new cutting and drying bed north of the barn to be sprayed for weeds; an order for limestone for the terrace; a reminder to the stone-carver about a new inscription.

I go back to writing, or trying to write. Into my review of a new book on the villas and gardens of the Roman author Pliny come the unwashed feet of the imagination asking about how some of this might find its way into Stonyground somewhere: an inscription? a planting? a design? How is all this related to the forum on landscape and its economies that I am to be part of in a month's time? How on earth did I drift into landscape architecture in the first place? What, above all, is Stonyground becoming, and what does the writing of this book say about what it has become?

And so it begins again, this cycle of the seasons that is always the same, and yet never the same. First, the desperate urgency of early-spring planting — more maples for the perimeter walks, perennials to add and move, the flats of seedling vegetables in the potting shed to be planted. And, all the while, even from late March, the early harbingers: snowdrops in the east lawn, blue and white scillas, and the brief purple beauty of the *Pulchella violacea*; great sheets of white crocus like late snow in the shrubbery beyond, and in the flowerbeds the white and purple hellebores and the bright flare of the little early tulips.

One day the grass is suddenly green, and the next, it seems, all the Darwin and lily-flowered and peony tulips are out at once. And then, before I have got their supporting baskets in place, the peonies are in bloom and the borders are lush with iris and alliums. The old apple trees on Barn Lawn are white with blossom, and the oriole is flashing his startling song.

By then the vegetable garden will have been manured and dug and planted. All that winter doodling on the printed plans is suddenly (usually in a day) there in little serried rows of fragile seedlings. And the potting shed has been emptied of its flats of plants once again and transformed into the summer dining-room. This is when all the visitors want to come, and as the open-day approaches, the Madonnas and the early lilies come, the astilbes and the dianthus and the sweet William, the little border phlox with the pink cranesbills and the larger purple ones, and the lupines in great rockets of colour — pink and cream and yellow and dark red.

"What do you hope that visitors will feel?" a friend asked me. I suppose it depends on the visitor. If they know

something about garden history, theirs will be the wryly
bemused pleasure of recognizing the various sorts of quota-
tions that the garden includes in its plantings, buildings, and
flowers. If they knew the place before I began, it will be
surprise, though one of my great pleasures comes when
visitors imagine that the garden has always been here, a
lucky inheritance. Sometimes, visitors tell me it is peace
that they feel. But mostly, I think, I would like them to feel
a catch in the throat at something they had always known
but forgotten; the lost garden at the back of an elusive
memory.

What the annual vistors rarely see, however, is the garden's comfortable middle age in high summer as the vast
cottage garden of the Great Garden fills up with hollyhocks
and helenium and helianthus, doronicum and the various
day lilies and lavatera, and the first lush, clovey scents of the
various colours of phlox. These are the nights when the
deep sweet scents stand like pools in the air, and things
seem to have been worth it after all.

And yet, as the first vegetables ripen in the *potager* — the
peas, and then the beans all in a rush — there is a melancholy too: "the barrenness of the fertile thing that can
achieve no more", as the American poet Wallace Stevens
says of this North American midsummer that is so unlike
the English one. Not that the often long and blissfully
insect-free autumns of southern Ontario do not have their
own beauties, even their own flowers — the chelones and
sedums and asters. But for me as a gardener it is a time of

short rations as I return to teaching. The moving of perennials and the planting of bulbs, and just the general maintenance of things that has to be squeezed into a shorter week. And my mind, which has spent the summer ranging over the fields and gardens, contracts itself to the task of "trying to make people who don't want to listen listen, and who don't want to see see" (as the writer Flannery O'Connor put it). It is short-order cooking after the gourmet buffet, but even in the dreariest grammar-correcting moments of teaching, the garden sneaks in with plans for a new corner or a different planting. And so the anticipation of the thing becomes, as with so many things, as good as the thing itself. "Let a bleak paleness chalk the door, so all within be livelier than before," said the poet George Herbert, both of winter and of old age. Yes, that's it, "livelier than before".

Legend

1. Chinese House
2. Hogarth Monument
3. Diana Stone
4. Hercules Plow
   (Site of Ceres Temple)
5. Memorial to my Mother
6. Ilium Memorial to my Aunt
7. Elgin Monument
8. Richard Wilson Inscription
9. 'Corinthian Porticos' *(Marvell)*
10. Dante Stone
11. Homage to Palmer
12. 'Woods' Monument
13. 'Satan began his pranks in a tree'
    (Traherne)
14. 'Harps' Stone
15. Column
16. 'I found the poems' *(Clare)*
17. 'Nature Abhors...' *(Kent)*
18. 'Erring'
19. Aboretum *(Proposed)*

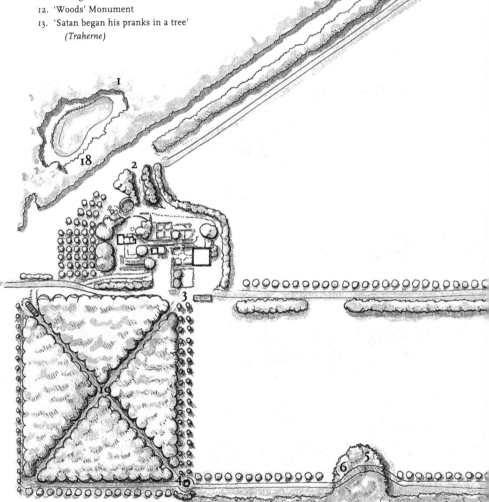

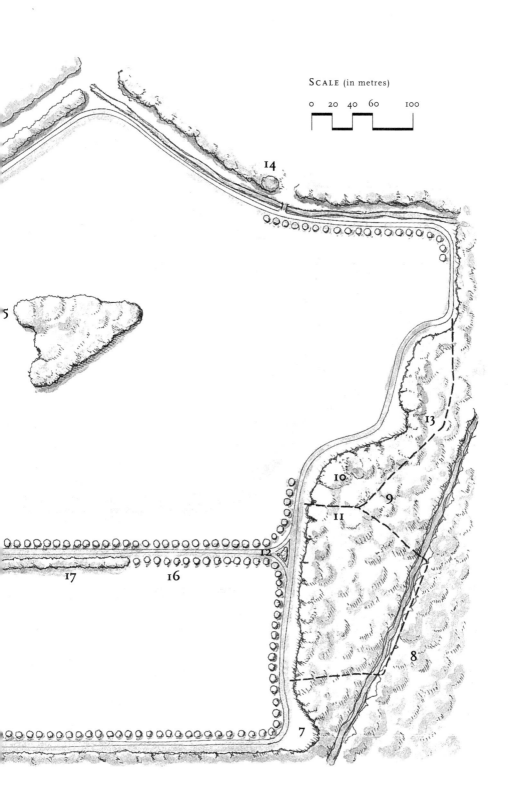

SCALE (in metres)

0   20   40   60   100

CHAPTER I

The Past

MIXING MEMORY AND DESIRE

Between Clifford and Mildmay on the southern border of
Bruce County, Ontario, just as the alluvial plain begins to
encounter the Singhamton moraine, the landscape begins
to fold and roll away and the Toronto radio stations fade
out. Here, on the same latitude as Belgrade and Bucharest
and Rimini and Toulouse, the rest of the world seems very
far away. One begins to catch glimpses of vistas like paintings by Carl Schaeffer, the Hanover artist who has made
this landscape his own. David Milne was born here, but this
is Schaeffer territory *par excellence*: undulating fields of
grain brooded over by storm. And in the middle of what is
some of the best farming country in southern Ontario —
twice the site of the International Plowing Match — is
Stonyground: a farm so heavily wooded that it was the last
lot in the township to be taken up from the Crown. And

yet its dense woods were a token of good soil, as are the fencerows of black walnuts that it still possesses. In this place, in 1984, I began to make a garden.

How does a garden begin ... with such a place, an idea, a favourite plant or group of plants, a design? Several of these come into the making of most gardens. Here, all of them played a part.

Planted with alfalfa, barley, wheat, soybeans, and corn, the farm's great fields stretch away northwest from the house and barn, rolling through a difference of thirty-five feet in elevation. This is "georgic" beauty, the beauty the Roman poet Virgil celebrated in his famous series of agricultural poems, *The Georgics*. It is a beauty of fields that stand so thick with corn that they laugh and sing, as the Psalmist says. And every year, from field to field the crops change, the views change, as they do throughout the seasons too: the early-spring dusting of vivid green to the giant dark green of the cornfields or the tawny luxuriance of the grains.

The fields now are enormous, a couple of them as big as fifty acres, as the sweep of ever-larger tractors demands a bigger canvas. But it was not so when I first knew the farm, as a boy fifty years ago. The fields then were still what a horse might work in a day, a horse with a single-furrow plough. That was all my great-uncle Angus would use: big, handsome Clydesdales with names like "Belle" and "Maude". Until I repaired the stable recently, their stalls were still in the barn; their harness still is.

Edging these old fields ran hedgerows that had grown up around the original split-rail fences: hedgerows of hawthorn and elm and wild apple. And in each field there were several stone piles — stones carried laboriously year after year in spring, or dragged by the horses on wooden stone-boats. Granite mostly, glacial till from the ice age, these stone piles also contained some of the subsoil limestone, full of trilobites and other mysterious creatures. One of my early treasures was a fossilized sponge. With the 1960s and big farm machinery, these stone piles were swept away to the margins of the property, and all but the perimeter hedgerows were grubbed out.

I know the effort with which each of these fields was originally cleared: the back-breaking chopping and dragging that destroyed my great-grandfather Duncan Campbell's health. To me as a child, though, these fields seemed ancient, mysterious enclosures, and the woods beyond even more mysterious. "Long, long ago," my great-aunt would say of the time of the clearing, as if it had happened centuries earlier and not (some of it anyway) within her own lifetime. Settlement and clearance seemed part of an epic story: the struggle against the wilderness preserved in the word "pioneers", a word that came from the army. In such an epic, individual heroic stories made perfect sense: my great-great-grandfather walking twenty miles to the nearest mill with a hundred-pound bag of grain and returning the same day because he had no money for a hotel. Or my great-grandfather walking a hundred miles to Buffalo to get medicine for his brother.

And so this was not an empty landscape, but one charged with powerful stories, like the ones my great-aunts would tell me around the butternut kitchen table on cool autumn weekends when Buck's Happy Thought Range warmed the room and baked the bread. Seamlessly these stories led back into a past that included Scotland and the emigration . . . or even the Scotland of the seventeenth century, the stories of the Covenanters. They were tales that could not be asked for. They came unprompted as the kettle steamed on the stove and the clock ticked in the corner.

And this was a legacy of a longer history: of the sense I got from the people who lived there of its place, not just in the history of the family, but in history itself. I think of my great-aunt telling me the name of the ship they sailed on from Scotland, and about her grandmother hiding under her cloak a young runaway from the press-gang who wanted to force him into the navy. Or another story about an ancestor in a remote part of Mull, a little boy who refused to tell the soldiers about a Covenanter and so had his arm broken by them. "I fancy that was before my time," she says on the tape that I once made of her, "in Charles II's reign."

Even my aunt, my mother's sister, who lived here all her life and taught English and history in the local high school, thought of this landscape of small farmers as no different from the ones that Virgil had written about. The country she knew was one where Cincinnatus could be called from the plough, one where high land taxes on the small farmer would lead as surely to the end of civilization as it did for the Romans.

Some of these stories would be about my great-uncle Angus. Taciturn and gaunt as a patriarch, it was hard to believe he had ever been the boy who took over the farm from his ailing father at the age of fifteen. In his eighties he had rebuilt the barn foundation. All the years of his life, he had heard the train go by — the train that crossed four times a day below the hill on which the farmhouse stands — and wished that he were on it, could "go west" like his brother. Often he lay on a cot by the stove, his dog and his stick nearby. All of this, this farm, this house, had come down to him and his two maiden sisters. *"Ne obliviscaris"* — "Do not forget" — was their motto, the motto of the Campbells. They did not.

Start with an old farm, then, my great-great-grand-father's farm . . . as far back on that side of the family as we go in this country, 1850 and the Crown grant. Or better still, start with my memories of stories about all this from these ancient great-aunts reciting Tennyson and Shelley in an old yellow-brick farmhouse, virtually unchanged since it was built in the 1870s. Surrounded by old maples, the garden had a long border that had run amok with hollyhocks and sweet rocket and peonies and Oriental poppies. These are my earliest memories from when I used to come to visit from the city. And these are what I remembered and doodled plans for over the many years in between.

Not long ago, as I moved a stone pile that contained a licence plate from 1968, I was reminded how recently the garden as it now is had been begun. The stone pile was near the barn and full of the old rubbish that farmers used to toss anywhere that seemed out of the way: local archaeology — old blue china, mysterious medicine bottles, long-forgotten tools and bits of implements. Now, many of them are the treasured stuff of memory. Some of the implements hang in the potting shed; the china goes to fill old quart glass jars to make lamp bases.

To our ancestors, the landscape, like the waterways, seemed inexhaustible. Even at Sissinghurst in early twentieth-century England, Vita Sackville-West had to clear some fifty old bathtubs from the forecourt of the former castle. Now, here, the plastic bags have to go to one part of the dump, the fence rails to another, and the barbed wire to a third. We see today, in all this disregarded familiar landscape, what was and is so precious just because we know how exhaustible it is. And Stonyground is as much about that recognition as it is about border planting and hedges. That stone pile was being moved so that a new part might be added to the garden: the barn ramp and plants to surround it. But its removal was also so that the farm wagons could more easily move in and out through this part of the garden, where at least one congenial location was to be a bench, made of old harrows and agricultural machinery, that would look out under old maples over ripening grainfields.

The bench is situated just as Gainsborough's is in the painting *Mr. and Mrs. Andrews:* looking out over a grainfield at the interchange of gentility and labour, gardening and harvesting. Gainsborough's couple claims possession.

Their bench is fashionably modern; Mrs. Andrews's dress is an assertion of their being literally and figuratively above the land they possess but do not work. The bench at Stonyground is for a different age, our own, conscious of the fragility of farming and our interchange with a threatened landscape, but able still, as Gainsborough's couple was, to see the working landscape as a beautiful place.

The mythology of Stonyground is not about possession but about the interchange that eighteenth-century gardeners saw between garden and landscape. "*Beatus satis ruris honoribus* ["It is enough to be blessed with the honours of the countryside"]," Lord Bolingbroke had inscribed around the front hall of his restored agricultural estate, Dawley Farm, when he rescued it from false gentrification in the 1730s. But it was Philip Southcote who first created at the same time what came to be known as a *ferme ornée* — Wooburn Farm in Surrey: a modest farm around and through which went walks planted with trees and shrubs and flowers, so that one could stroll through a farm in a garden and enjoy the beauties of horticulture and agriculture together.

Literally beautiful too, not sublime or picturesque, this rolling farmland of southern Ontario needs to be *looked* at again. It is where we are, where this garden is, and its gentle undulations are what the poet Alexander Pope called the "borrowed landscape" of the garden. The garden's pleasures are as much in the vistas out into my farmland, and my neighbours', as in its interior spaces. In those interchanges are the real questions about what a garden is: where we are, who we are now.

This, then, is where I began: not with the notion of making symmetrical gardens around the house (what in fact has come to be), but of making a walk around and through this working farm — a place from which to observe the beauties of the crops in their different seasons, the changing light and colour, the woods seen from different angles, the planted structures of the garden to be looked back at and not simply out from.

That first day, in April 1984, I walked over the furrowed fields, reciting Wallace Stevens's long poem "Credences of Summer" like some sort of litany or incantation:

Now in midsummer come and all fools slaughtered
And spring's infuriations over and a long way
To the first autumnal inhalations, young broods
Are in the grass, the roses are heavy with a weight
Of fragrance and the mind lays by its trouble.

And so the walks were begun, or rather (at first) the main avenue to the woods set out with transplanted maples . . . and then the path that picked up from it and wandered off through the tall deciduous trees, down into the denser cedars. I had forgotten (until I looked at my fitful journal for that year) that I had also begun to plant up two old intersecting fencerows that had escaped clearance. Now, as I write this, they have become a triangular grove midway

The Gainsborough bench

Bloodroot in bloom in the early spring fencerow

into one of the views of the farm from the house. Called a "spinney" because it is primarily a shelter for wildlife and can be reached only when the crop has been taken off the fields, it has the mysterious quality of an ancient place seldom approached: not even part of the peripheral walks that I had been planning.

Anyone who has ever walked in a farm in southern Ontario knows that the landscape has its own garden: bloodroot and dog-tooth violets (or trout lilies) in spring, and oxeye daisies, blue-eyed grass, and buttercups in early summer; and later, Queen Anne's lace and clover, the little wild snapdragon commonly called "toadflax", the two mallows pink and white, and the lovely intense yellow of bird's-foot trefoil, black-eyed Susans, goldenrod (which the gardeners call *Solidago* to gentrify it), common mullein . . . and in the damp spots, the wild anemone and blue and red lobelias and Joe-Pye weed and the wild white chelone. So gardening is a matter of simply adding things that are congruent, and hardy enough to deal with all those foreign weeds that are (like many of our so-called native plants and birds), in fact, imports: evidence of our longing for "home" and elsewhere.

Sometime within the first two centuries of settlement, American immigrants from Britain stopped thinking of themselves as Englishmen living abroad and began to consider themselves natives of the continent where they lived. For us, in southern Ontario, it is getting on for those two hundred years. Perhaps we can now accept who we are and where:

what Northrop Frye called "Americans who rejected the revolution" but inhabitants of this continent nonetheless. We can celebrate its ordinary agricultural heroism (our real history) as well as the stuff that gets set apart in plaqued historic enclaves.

My love of this place, and what I have done, is also in gratitude for that history, for all that was done for me against terrific odds: my great-great-grandfather walking into the wilderness, carrying the sickle that he had bought when he got off the boat in Quebec, a sickle that I still have. Or my great-uncle planting a purple beech (which he would have had to buy) before he had finished clearing the trees from the land. Everything I do now, these gardens and walks, are what they might have done had they had my time and the leisure; indeed, I am what they became, and the garden and landscapes are in that sense theirs.

It is easy to fall into moony mysticism about all this, especially when you can lie out under the stars (as I did with some friends on that first August night of San Lorenzo in 1984) and watch the meteors falling like fireworks over a just-harvested barleyfield. But it would be equally strange not to be haunted by it. "Consult the genius of the place in all," Pope wrote to his friend Lord Burlington about laying out his estate. Surely what he meant has to include, not only the nature of the topography, but the life that has been lived within it, its dense associations with people as well as its geology.

Frequently a trick of light or a shadow suggests that someone else is there. I think of times when I am chopping wood and have the sense of my clumsiness being watched, not altogether uncritically, by some forbear. And once, I remember picking cherries in a wild tree on the east fence-line and feeling intensely that a woman in a long print dress and a large bonnet — my great-grandmother, perhaps — was looking up at me: curious at what she had become.

Shaped by stories and legends as much as by the literal stuff of felling and cultivation, Stonyground is for me as much a mythical place as "New Moon" in the *Emily* books of Lucy Maude Montgomery. It is what I came back to Canada for from a teaching career in England at a time when the Cold War still threatened the end of everything: the place at the end of time. The phrase is Yeats's and it was Yeats who gave me its name, from his "Meditations in Time of Civil War":

An ancient bridge, and a more ancient tower,
A farmhouse that is sheltered by its wall,
An acre of stony ground.

And I suppose that is also why (though I did not think so at the time) I later made in the garden a monument to the end of the Cold War: what I called an *"ara pacis"* after the great Altar of Peace that the Emperor Augustus made in Rome to celebrate the universal peace that he had imposed upon the Empire, the same peace that Pope's contemporaries thought they were creating by calling themselves "Augustans". Mine is a modest monument: a stone plinth the size of a sundial surmounted by a mould-board (the last part of a ploughshare), and with the text from Isaiah, "*gladios in vomeres*" ("swords into ploughshares").

There it stands, at the end of the hedge-on-sticks walk that is the spine of the garden and just at the moment when the garden-walker mounts the steps of native lime-stone and looks out, from the terrace by the barn, over the whole of the farm: the larger landscape that the visitor is now invited to consider and to walk through. The hedge-on-sticks came last or almost last — last on the ini-tial plan, certainly — of all the parts of the garden round the house. It is made of littleleaf lindens kept trimmed (above shoulder height to about fifteen feet): hence the name. Now it looks as if it were what made the rest hap-pen, but that was not so.

What came first were some essential repairs to the house and barn. There was no point trying to garden until those "bones" had been set to rights, as Harold Nicolson under-stood at Sissinghurst. Whenever Vita Sackville-West planted flowers before the walks and borders had been properly made, he pulled the flowers out. I suppose a feminist would spot the testosterone factor in all this: the male's desire to leave his mark rather than to nurture. Perhaps as I sink into middle age I become happier with gardening and less demanding in my plans. I wonder.

Although I had still not formulated a plan for the gar-dens around the house, it was already clear that whatever went there needed to be properly prepared and laid out.

The barn, which was later to be the dominant feature of the Great Garden, had its posts (the supporting pillars) set upright again, and the house had repairs to the brick west wall, which had bowed out from an insubstantial foundation. More essential: although the house had a bathroom, my mystification as to why it also had an outdoor privy (which was still there when I came) was dispelled when I discovered that the bathroom was only for "show" (like many on the Greek islands) and that there was no septic tank.

West of the house, where there had been a vegetable garden in my childhood, was now a wilderness of small maples, some of which had been dug up and transplanted into the avenue to the woods: an avenue that was to replace the old farm lane that had largely been grubbed up by my uncles who had been farming the place. Oh, and there was lilac run wild too: my dear friend Myra singing "We'll murder lilacs in the spring" as we hacked and dug away in the howling March wind. Two springs' worth of maples had been moved, but now a wholesale attack on this "wilderness" behind the house was necessary to install the septic tank. And so, almost at a stroke, the west lawn was dug up, levelled, and laid.

In the midst of all this — and of having a new lane made and the crumbled walls of the old kitchen repaired — came my first visitors: old friends from New York. No proper kitchen, no functioning bathroom, bulldozers and excavators, and then a colossal electrical storm. "What is going on?" said Judith.

What is surprising is that the plans these friends urged me to set down are largely the ones I ultimately realized. At that stage I committed nothing to paper, but I can see now that something of the first master plan was beginning to form. What is different in what came to be made (apart from the breathless optimism) is the plan for ponds and water generally, but more of that later. By then, though, I had also begun to learn two things: the abrupt immediacy of the natural world and the strangeness of local life and speech.

Local usage was the more difficult, to begin with. In my journal for that year there is a page of clippings from *The Walkerton Herald-Times:* "Majority in Favour of Capital Pun.", "Squirt Boys End Losing Streak", "Hit By Tree Proton Man Is Improving", "Happy Hookers Standing Pat". Plainly this was a place of occult speech. I thought of the Irish expression: "If you wanted to get there you wouldn't want to start from here." In those early days I still did not drive. "You're going to Trawna tomorrow?" asked my aunt, when I was taking the bus one weekend. "Well, I expect you'd like a ride to the bus." I said I would, only to be told, "Well, you do what you like."

Even now, ten years later, local manners and customs can be bewildering. Contractors who did a recent job for me had still not given me a bill for it six months later, and declined to do so until they got in their subcontractors' bills. When the bill finally did arrive, it was nearly 60 per cent higher than the estimate, but plainly it was "not done" to question such things. On the other hand, there was the matter of the barn repairs in that first year. Fifty years of neglect had left it with a distinct lean to the east. Thanks to the absence of cattle (and hence, heating), the barn ramp on the west side had gone on freezing and thawing every year, and so pushing the structure out of true. "Do you think you can fix it?" I said to the old boy who was the local expert. "Waal," he said, "it might cost you a thousand dollars." In the end it cost four hundred. Welcome to the world of Jean de Florette!

Nature, too, was a different text: squirrels who conducted the third world war each morning in the spruce trees near the house, and groundhogs who had mined the hill where the house sits and were in no mind to shift. At one time I thought of writing an account of my early adventures called "Bats in the Attic, Snakes in the Cellar", but it would have been poor competition for another ad in the local newspaper: "*One Foot in the Furrow* by Bob Trotter".

Autumn comes all too quickly; each year my record contains a lament for the need to leave just when things are at the "season of mists and mellow fruitfulness". Slow goings-away of everything . . . and then the clean-up . . . and winter. And such winter as I had forgotten — the winters of my childhood, coming up on the steam train from Toronto and being met by my uncle in a sleigh filled with buffalo robes because the roads were not kept ploughed: a memory as distant and magical as something out of *Anna Karenina*.

The snow was up to the telephone wires, and the house (my grandmother's house close by) steamed with the constant kettle on the woodstove: waking at dawn to its early smell and the sound of the hand-turned milk separator, for this was even before the coming of electricity. Even now, friends who have been to visit Stonyground in the cool weather call up like pilgrims weeks later to marvel that their clothes still smell of woodsmoke.

What has this to do with the making of the place — except that memory is also a powerful maker? It stays like an unappeasable hunger demanding to be satisfied. Here, then, was satisfaction, or the beginning of it: a farm sheeted over with snow, the silver-grey of the hawthorn hedges, the high bright blue of the distinctive intense winter sky. And a snowfall like those I could only dimly remember: all day and all night. And then the roads closed and a great and universal peace. We went for a walk to the woods on snow-shoes, floundering like kids in a millpond until we got into the ice palace of the trees, where the wind ceased and the quiet was audible. Coming out again, we found suddenly a howling storm and not even your hand in front of your face visible . . . so that only staggering from one of the newly planted maples to the next got us back up the lane to the house, reeling with exhaustion, only inches from what Emily Dickinson called "first chill, then stupor, then the letting go".

A good lesson. It is easy to sentimentalize the country: to forget about the tree that twists suddenly and falls the wrong way, trapping you miles from anyone who might be concerned enough to look, or the rock for a wall that is just too big and torques back, trapping your foot. Agriculture is still the most dangerous occupation. My farming cousin, Campbell, has three stubby fingers as a record of an absent-minded intervention with some silage machinery. Making a garden in the country has some of those dangers too, as my scarred hands and gammy back will witness. Old pieces of glass lurk in the flowerbeds, or a piece of rusty barbed wire in the underbrush to be cleared. But some bravado takes you on: a crazed fundamentalist belief in the rightness of it that draws you out in February (when the garden cannot be damaged by falling branches) to cut down some of the still-too-many trees that are turning your semi-shade into mere gloom.

"Can it be true," I find myself having written in the journal for that year, "that Titian did not begin to paint until he was fifty?" Well, I was not fifty yet, though many times since I have wished that I could have started all this when I was younger. I have a desperate fear of running out of steam and enthusiasm. No such worry in 1984, when the vegetable garden was already in the planning stages and the eastern walk (not to be realized until 1990) was already part of the overall plan.

Ten years later, from the superior hindsight of computer technology, all of this record, retrieved from memory and notebooks kept after exhausting (and frequently depressing) days, seems a little fuzzy. What comes across is dogged determination, and odds that seemed less than fair and certainly more daunting than I would care to face now.

CHAPTER 2

ORDERING THE WILDERNESS
THE POTAGER

The first of the gardens near the house was the *potager*, the vegetable garden, begun in the spring of 1985. "Olitory gardens," John Evelyn called them, and he devoted a whole section to them in "Elysium Britannicum", his great unpublished work on gardens. *Acetaria*, the part on salads, was published separately and contains one of the great recipes for salad dressing:

> *Your herbs being handsomly parcell'd, and spread on a clean napkin before you, are to be mingl'd together in one of the earthen glaz'd dishes. Then, for the Oxoleon; take of clear, and perfectly good oyl-olive, three parts; of sharpest vinegar (sweetest of all condiments), limon, or juice of orange, one part; and therein let steep some slices of horse-radish, with a little salt. Some in a separate vinegar, gently bruise a pod of Guinny-*

pepper, straining both the vinegars apart, to make use of either, or one alone, or of both, as they best like; then add as much Tewkesbury, or other dry mustard grated, as will lie upon an half-crown piece. Beat and mingle all these very well together; but pour not on the oyl and vinegar 'till immediately before the sallet is ready to be eaten; and then with the yolk of two new-laid eggs (boyl'd and prepar'd) squash and bruise them all into mash with a spoon; and lastly, pour in all upon the herbs, stirring and mingling them 'till they are well and thoroughly imbib'd; not forgetting the sprinkling of aromaticks, and such flowers as we have already mentioned, if you think fit, and garnishing the dish with thin slices of horse-radish, red beet, berberries, &c.

Note, That the liquids may be made more or less acid, as is most agreeable to your taste.

Every spring come the seed-lists from local nurseries, offering irresistible curiosities for the vegetable gardener: a cross between celery and lettuce, a purple broccoli, or red Brussels sprouts. 'Tis "the season of lists and callow hopefulness," said the garden writer Katherine White, parodying Keats. I prefer Dr. Johnson's description of second marriage: "the triumph of hope over experience". Never mind, it is irresistible. Even a recent catalogue from a botanical bookseller, I notice, has a section on "olericulture".

My vegetable garden is called by its French name because it is a poor-man's imitation of the most elegant French vegetable garden, the one on the Loire at Villandry. And it is also a re-creation of the earliest vegetable gardens in Canada: the *jardins potager* of the Fortress of Louisbourg in Nova Scotia. The idea came to me, though, from the garden writer Rosemary Verey: her wonderful vegetable garden at Barnsley in Gloucestershire. There, the French ideas are modified and softened, but the essential principles are still present: a mixture of flowers and vegetables planted for texture and colour as well as for use; an elaborate pattern of small beds that need never be walked on; brick walks, and a hedge enclosure.

Every house in the country needs a vegetable garden. I started to make mine on what I remembered was the site of the original henyard (hence, fertile soil): need overlaid with memory. What was there was a jungle of brambles and little trees and rubbish. So it was begun, with a rototiller and a plan: fifty feet square, four quadrants of differing designs with brick paths, and at the centre a roundel where, as Yeats says, "the symbolic rose can break in flower". In this case it does so through a cartwheel up-ended on its axle: the rose of eternity growing through the wheel of time. And just to keep the solemnity in perspective, it's all placed in the midst of a bed of lemon thyme.

Like many of these things here, though, to think of the *potager* now is to wonder how it was ever started. Paths four feet wide had to be dug down three feet (this is Canada and serious frost, not England) and filled with gravel and sand before the bricks could be laid. And though I say "bricks", these were, of course, lock-stone (brick breaks up in the ground in this climate), though not the horrible wavy ones, and of a colour that matched the old yellow brick of the house some fifty feet away.

In such a plan, the soil (manured annually from my farming cousin's abundant supply) remains friable, and everything can be planted more densely than in most vegetable gardens. Here, too, near the house, on top of a drumlin that is the end of the Singhamton moraine, the soil is sandy loam. And at least forty years of neglect (my predecessor, my great-aunt, was ninety-nine when she died) had added leaf and apple mould.

Recently we have been digging post-holes for the last gate into the *potager*. After several years of groundhog invasion, I had decided to fence it with a wire mesh that I believed — rightly, as it turned out — would be invisible in the hedge of raspberries that surrounds the garden. The post-holes confirmed what I believed all along, a soil that couldn't be better: two feet of wonderful loam on top of the sandy gravel of the drumlin.

But what did I, a professor of English, know about constructing garden paths? Oh, I had gardened as a child with my father in the thankless clay of North Toronto, but nothing on this scale: a little knowledge about annuals and perennials, and enough about hybrid tea roses to make me determined never to grow them here: that was all. And I had started to write garden history, but not of the kind that taught you how to double-dig a border or lay out a vegetable garden. Fortunately I had a friend, a landscape architect, who knew about garden construction. So we began the back-breaking work. The heaviest slog of any of the gardens, it's just as well the *potager* came first.

But I had scarcely begun when this not-even-yet-garden said to me: "You don't expect me to be here by myself, do you? I look ridiculous on my own." The first circle in the centre made the landscape surround it, like a new order, a new way of seeing things. And there, suddenly, were all the questions about nature and art — their relation to each other — that have gone on being the most interesting part of what I have been doing.

"Do you think what you're doing is natural?" my ecological friends ask me, as if the "nature" of Bruce County had not been radically interfered with long ago by man's preoccupations. Even the First Nations, the Huron and (later) Ojibwa who stalked these woods, introduced vegetables and cultivation to it. And it was they who named plantain, that common lawn weed, "white man's foot" in recognition of its foreign origins. And so with much of the "nature" that we treasure: by now (like us humans) so hybridized with the rest as to be virtually unretrievable in origin. The American garden writer Michael Pollan has argued in his book, *Second Nature,* that the desire to re-create an unviolated wilderness is a pipe-dream of those who have never stopped to think that the spectator within such a landscape already carries the mental and physical seeds of its alteration.

Whatever "was here" was so in a way long removed from the wilderness clichés of Disney films. There are beaver in the stream in my woods as I write this, but I can find no evidence that there had been any here since European settlement, and in fact I suspect that they are here now as a result of the

An early aerial view of the *potager* from the house

disappearance of predators. Bears have long been gone too, though there is a family story from more than a hundred years ago of my great-uncle as a little boy coming home from fetching the cows and saying that he had seen "a big black pig up in the trees, breaking branches".

As for wolves, there have not been any of those for a long time either, though rumours persist that the Greenock Swamp (the huge wetland that runs through the southern part of the county, west of my farm) is full of them. In fact, in it primarily are packs of "coy-dogs": western coyotes that have come east in the United States, and so up here, and have mated with wild dogs. Local farmers, enraged by their talent for taking sheep, recently held a meeting to deal with these "wolves", at which a nature-lady from Toronto objected that all that was necessary was to castrate the males. Rising shakily to his feet, a grizzled ninety-year-old suggested that she'd missed the point. "Lady," he said, "these wolves ain't screwing our sheep, they're eating them."

So much for nature and art! But art is nowhere more obvious than in the nice regularities of the *potager*, its fifty-five or so vegetables ordered by texture and colour and shape. Many different types of lettuces line the edges of the beds; the taller beans and brassicas stand behind; and in the midst are the staked and trellised tomatoes and peas. As the season progresses, the flowering kales and cabbages on the main cross-paths hide the kitchen depredations, and broccoli and borecole rise up in the place of the earlier summer vegetables.

Are the nasturtiums that line the centre roundel there as insect deterrents, as decoration, or as salad ingredients? Well, all three; and is not the desire to separate these things an index of what is the matter with much gardening — the desire for closure and neatness and discreteness? My mother used to pop tomato plants in behind my father's border roses, to his suburban-gardener annoyance. But tomatoes were originally thought of as decorative — and why not now?

In his wonderful novel *An Imaginary Life*, the Australian writer David Malouf invented the life of the Roman poet Ovid in exile on the Black Sea. Unable to speak to the villagers, who have no Latin, Ovid finds himself teaching a wild boy who has been raised by wolves. From him, in turn, Ovid relearns something that he had forgotten — the wild knowledge that he and his brother had had as boys, when they played with the foxes in his father's vineyards. And so the literate learns from the illiterate. The interchange of the wild and the tame, life at the borders of knowledge, translations: these are what gardening is also about, if one is not to poison the vegetables with pesticide, on the one hand, or let the wild clematis overwhelm the raspberries, on the other. The *potager* re-establishes this dialogue, this debate about the respective roles of nature and art.

Although the *potager* was made and planted that spring, already it demanded more, and so the gardens around it began to suggest themselves. Looking now at my old photographs of the site, strewn with decaying machinery, brambles, and stone piles, and covered with coarse gravel, I wonder how my madness

The *potager* as it now is showing the wheel of time and looking through
one of the portals towards the house

prevailed over what was largely an agricultural junk-heap, but it did.

First of all, though, there were other major undertakings around the house to be seen to. Although the heating (beyond the wonderfully efficient old woodstove) was entirely electric, my great-aunt had only a sixty-amp service. This meant that, if you turned on a heater in more than one room in the house, the whole service blew. So, there was the garden upheaval of a major new (underground) electrical service to be installed before the lawns and borders could be made.

And beyond them, in the meadow to the south, between the house and the road, the first beginnings of an orchard of old-fashioned apples and pears were laid out. "Ort-yard" or "hortyard": the great garden reformers of the seventeenth century thought of fruit-growing especially as the return to paradise. For Milton, unfallen Eden was a place where Adam and Eve engaged in "rural work" in the orchard:

> *Among sweet dews and flow'rs; where any row*
> *Of Fruit-trees overwoody reach'd too far*
> *Their pamper'd boughs, and needed hands to check*
> *Fruitless imbraces: or they led the Vine*
> *To wed her Elm; she spous'd about him twines*
> *Her marriageable arms, and with her brings*
> *Her dow'r th' adopted Clusters, to adorn*
> *His barren leaves. . . .*

Milton's contemporary Ralph Austen was even more explicit in his *A Treatise of Fruit Trees:*

> *God, who is wisdome it selfe; says that a* Garden of Fruit-trees *was the meetest place upon all the Earth for* Adam *to dwell in, even in his state of perfection . . .* Augustin *[St. Augustine] is of opinion, that this* dressing of the Garden, *was as well an exercise of the hand, as of the mind, not with toylesomeness and trouble, but with delight and pleasure.*

Well, perhaps not always, not anyway as one tries in a frantic rush each spring to plant the new trees bare-root in the brief time in which that's possible. This orchard was to replace the one that I remembered being there and from which only a solitary "Duchess" apple-tree remained. Moving down year by year towards the road, the rows of old-fashioned pears and apples were not only to replace the orchard that had once been there but (more important) to hide the road, filter the noise, and carry the eye from the house, across the tops of fruit trees, into the woods on the other side.

Now, as I write this, I think more and more about the need for quiet: the great hunger for it that comes from living in a world full of incident noise. How blissful it is when a snowfall clogs the roads and the only sound is the wind! And I begin to dream about an arboretum that will blot out the neighbour's house five hundred feet away, and the machine shop beyond it. Will I live long enough to see any of this mature? I wonder.

Of course, this planting was (and is) another sort of madness. What will I do with the fruit of fifty or sixty trees? I'll have to offer free pick-your-own to all comers. It's the *look* of the thing: a sea of apple blossom in the spring like those wonderful compositions by the early twentieth-century Ontario photographer Reuben Sallows that I was later to discover. But none of it was easy. In the inhospitable gravel of that drumlin field, the trees are taking their own sweet time to mature . . . those that have made it past the rabbits and the frost, that is. And in the beginning there was the usual argument about whether it was better not to manure and so to let the trees cope with the poor soil there to begin with. They would then set deeper roots, so the argument goes. It's a rerun of the "to stake or not to stake" argument. I think now, with hindsight, I'd say "yes" to both.

I'd also say, from bitter experience: Make sure to put collars on the trees. And not those silly little wrap-around useless things either, but white plastic drainage-tile collars. (You can't use the less visible black tile for fear of "cooking" the trees in the hot weather.) These are collars that even the manic jackrabbit who girdled half of my orchard one February night could not get through. Of course, such collars may also provide a nesting-box for girdling mice (the collars are a devil to put on as well), but there's a limit to preventive medicine. Even for the maples we came to find collars necessary. A hungry rabbit or a porcupine will go for maple bark as readily as a marauding white-tailed deer: the sort that came out of my woods the second winter to attack the newly planted trees.

Naturally, though, I look forward to the day when these ugly white prophylactics come off the trees.

This business of usable tools and equipment is one of the bugbears of gardeners. How many pairs of useless little gardener's knee-pads did I go through before I discovered that what was wanted was the tough rubber ones that floorers use when installing hardwood and tile. Why do nurseries not sell those nice long-handled spades that builders use for forming concrete? Small-bladed and adaptable, they are ideal for getting a tough burdock out of a tight corner. And they are far better for planting little bulbs than those maddening bulb-plug mechanisms that either refuse to release the soil or drop it back in the hole before you can retrieve it!

We continued this spring to extend the avenue of transplanted maples to the woods. My poor friend Myra, not inoculated by one April of mud and lilacs, came back for another of tree-wrestling in the howling winds . . . only to fall headlong into a furrow with a scream as we were on our walk. A path about twenty feet wide had been taken back from the fields, not just for the central avenue, but for the perimeter walk around the farm. Now there was the business of connecting them all, and of making a walk through the woods as part of that circuit. "Oh," said one of my historical friends, as we went at the sapling with saws and pruning shears, "I feel as if I'm building the Huron Road." I reminded him that John Galt hadn't used garden tools.

That summer a ginger cat wandered in, a charmer who would sit on my shoulder as I walked about, and talk in my ear. Fortunately he was fond of cars and would jump in like a dog at the least suggestion of a trip, and sit there contentedly. Just as well, as that summer I had to go back and forth every week to Toronto. Teaching summer school at the university, I could garden only at weekends, when I also planned a tour of English gardens that I was to take in the autumn, during a half-sabbatical.

The tour, it turned out, was to gel a number of ideas about garden plans that were still free-floating in my mind: half-remembered gardens that I had liked in England, bits from here and there. By then, having drifted out of writing a book on Milton and a curiosity about his inspiration for the description of Eden's garden in *Paradise Lost*, I had begun to think about a book on the planters of the great English gardens of the late seventeeth and early eighteenth centuries. And from that I had gone on to become interested in John Evelyn, one of the great gardeners and garden historians of that period.

So I went to England with my little group in the autumn, among them one who was to become a great gardening friend. No mean gardener herself, Dorothy had a wonderful town garden in Goderich that came to be as much a supply of plants for Stonyground as she herself was a well of enthusiasm. The group also included two landscape-architect friends, and so we were already looking for ideas and reminders. As we went round the thirty or so gardens that we saw in those three weeks in September, ideas for a pavilion came from Hidcote, a seat from Rousham, a hedged garden enclosure from Sissinghurst, the need for an overall landscape program from Stowe, and so on. And throughout the trip, every evening over dinner, we talked about how all this might be "translated" into the vocabulary of Stonyground.

For all gardening is a kind of translation — of ideas, plants, plantings, plans — and an attempt to respect "the genius of the place": to get it right, rarely so in the first place. What is it that they wanted, the people who founded this place? What do their evidences suggest: their trees and their plants and what is left of their flowerbeds? And out of other gardens, even ones centuries gone, come ideas for hedges, spaces, seats, monuments, plantings — even interchanges with the surrounding landscape. One looks at old plans and prints or finds historical accounts in memoirs and letters, such as Mrs. Delany's wonderful descriptions of the eighteenth-century gardens she knew in Ireland. Or one reads of gardens in fiction: some of them hilarious warnings, such as Wemmick's bower in *Great Expectations*, or emotionally powerful, as "the red deeps" in *The Mill on the Floss*.

Much of my garden-making has also been a matter of cooperation and consultation. For all that Stonyground is my garden, I am greatly indebted to friends for interventions small and large: to one who suggested stripping up the lower branches of the trees behind the house to "call in" the long view from there, for instance, or to another who suggested a flight of steps down the hill and set about to make them.

I stayed in England to do some research. Ron Fischer (one of my landscape-architect friends) went home and drew up a plan out of what we had talked about. That winter was full of dreamy plans, inspired by my also teaching a course in garden history to some of the college alumnae/i. Gradually things began to unfold: a garden (what was to be the Great Garden) next to the barn, with a smaller oval garden to connect it through an arbour to the rebuilt pump-house; hedges of trimmed pine to surround it all; a walk between all this side of the garden and the *potager* to the west, a walk to serve as the garden's spine and bring everything into an illusion of order; walls and gravelled walks to provide the garden's "bones". This — 1986 — was to be the first year of major assault on the garden.

CHAPTER 3

A Basket of Flowers

The Great Garden

It started in a minor enough way, the season of '86: next to the house, a patio in the same lock-stone as the *potager*, with a pergola that was to be the model for a number of later arbours. From it a new path leading through the *potager* to the site of the old henhouse, a site that was to be transformed into a compost yard, with a nursery facing it underneath an old apple tree on the other side of the path. That was early summer, when I was also making the car park that was to be adjacent to the Great Garden, fashioned from the stone picked from the fields by the machine invented by some other cousins: an astonishing thing of rakes and flywheels and rotating drums. The stone went into the car-park site, and over it gravel, and a little bit of order came in.

Machines on this scale were a new thing to me, and

much of my subsequent career at Stonyground has involved getting used to them . . . never entirely successfully. As I write this chapter on a violent winter day in February, when the storm has closed all the roads in the county for two days, I rejoice in the power of nature to call all the arrogant patriarchal noise-making of our culture to a halt. And I remember now that that is how I felt as a child. Here at last was something that could stop the adults and their smug complacency about the engineering of the world.

It must have been in that summer of 1986, nonetheless, that I first got hold of a man with a stump-grinder — a machine that makes short work of what might otherwise have taken years to rot away. And that must also have been the year that I got an old Ford–Ferguson tractor: one of the little stubby grey jobs that I had driven as a boy hauling wagons piled with sheaves. My dreams of having all sorts of horticultural gizmos to go with it remain just that, but it's worth having it just to take friends' children for a ride. I wish I could feel as kindly towards post-hole–diggers, those wreckers of necks and backs!

First there was the pergola, and even before that another piece of back-breaking as we levelled a terrace behind the house for it, using the same "bricks" as for the *potager.* Here, where a jungle had been only a couple of years earlier, it became possible to contemplate the garden and the view: a place to hoist a martini, as other gardeners have been known to do. My landscape-architect friend Ron engineered the footings for the cedar posts and worked the foundations cunningly around an old disused cistern, and the day of triumph came when the last "gull-wing" ornament went on. Prospect and ease: every garden should have someplace for these.

Every garden should have stages too: to allow both for time in which to have second thoughts and for the satisfaction of accomplishment. Every year needs something. And every year also needs a place that is inviolate, not a scene of mud and confusion. I have known more than one marriage to come unstuck over house renovations that left nowhere as a refuge from the plaster dust, no comfortable chair in a corner for reading.

It was also in the spring of '86 that we demolished the old garage: a hideous thing of green insulbrick whose apparent flimsiness belied the enormously heavy barn timbers that had been laid to make its foundation. Like many a load of old rubbish since, it went into the gravel pit on the west face of the hill on which the house stands: a pit that I originally intended to fill in but that still (ten years later) is the site of annual bonfires of the year's combustible rubbish: an essential element of a garden like this.

It was that spring, too, that the herb garden proper was made. I had planted one previously at the end of an old bed, but the new one was to become a feature on the path to the *potager*, turning the walk to a right angle with one side of its hexagon. Nearer to the house than the *potager*, this garden was for the quick dashes that cooks make for some last-minute herb: chives and parsley and thyme and savory for the cooking, and, for the salads, arugula, lovage, tarragon, fennel, sorrel, coriander, and basil. Every year I become impatient for the June Herb Fair in Durham, twenty miles away, and so I buy the annual herbs first from the nursery. But then the Herb Fair comes, and I find myself jamming in twice as much again.

In the middle of the herb garden, then, I put in a marten house: the beginning of my (still futile) attempts to attract a colony of those avid mosquito-eaters. The marten scouts had a look but sounded as if they had decided that there were not enough bathrooms . . . or garages. Birds here, though, are one of the great mysteries and delights. One early autumn morning, as I was working at my desk, a ruffed grouse flew in a fury at his reflection in the window. But more usually there are goldfinches, buntings, orioles, bobolinks, and even (latterly) those foreign sweet singers, the house finches that can out-coloratura even the song sparrows and the whitethroats. I have just (at last) got round to making a bird-bath for them, but they seem to have been undeterred by the inconvenience in the meantime.

The eminent Victorian garden writer Canon Ellacombe had no faith in fixed plans for gardens, but there are many dangers that lie in wait for those who trust to instinct. The wonderful Irish novelist Molly Keane has described some splendid gardens, but none is more memorable than the cat-astrophic garden of Aunt Louisa in her novel *Full House:*

*This garden was designed with all the ingenuity of a
formless mind. There was something almost invigorating in
its awful failure to please. The whole thing was really the
most stupendous failure. There was nothing about it that
anybody could possibly commend. Even Aunt Louisa wondered about it a little at times, but she would still any
query in her mind by buying another pot of stone or
alabaster and disposing it in some fresh nook.*

Such are the dangers that lie in wait for the gardener of
"inspirations". (Second thoughts are something else altogether.) Hernias are a common danger for (at least male)
gardeners too. One of the lesser surgeries for them involves
a "butterfly bandage" that frequently fails to work. Radical
surgery with stitches is the only sure intervention. So it is
with gardens. Nothing half-hearted will do.

The third of June was a banner day that year: the day
when "Granny" Taylor arrived with his little bulldozer and
began to shape what was to be the Great Garden. As the
name suggests, this was to be the largest of the gardens: the
major statement terminating what was to be the vista down
the main walk from the house. Made out of what had been
the turn-around for the farm wagons at the barn, it
required getting rid of great quantities of gravel and levelling up a site that sloped as much as three feet to the east.
There, a wall had to be built from some usefully squared
old barn granite, and the whole thing was to be hedged
with seedling white pines.

Laying out the walks, beds and fountain in
the first stage of the Great Garden

Previous page The pergola by the house covered
with porcelain berry and clematis

48

The Great Garden, as designed by Ron, was to be square to the barn that it would abut — like the *potager* a square, but a sixty-foot square — again divided into quadrants by wide gravel walks, but this time the beds would be of perennials in four different colours: pink going to red, and yellow going to orange. Edged with four-inch rectangular pieces of limestone ledgerock, this garden is filled at the centre with *Artemisia lactiflora*: a handsomer version of the common *Artemisia* that goes by the unhandsome name of mugwort.

"A fine plant grown in a mass in a semi-wild garden," says the Royal Horticultural Society's *Dictionary of Gardening* about *Artemisia lactiflora*, and so it is a good edging to what now looks like an enormous overgrown cottage garden. An overflowing basket of flowers, the sort of garden flowers that such a farm as this might have had originally, this garden was inspired by the greatest of the twentieth-century English gardeners, Gertrude Jekyll, as she in turn had been inspired by the cottage gardens of West Surrey: the sort of gardens that turn up in the paintings and illustrations of Helen Allingham.

The Great Garden is the antithesis of what I call the "brown-earth school of gardening": everything neatly set off by its little patch of safely dead earth. Certainly it is no place for gardening nannies: hair well brushed and fingernails clean. As blowsy and sluttish as its Oriental poppies and peonies, the Great Garden looks as if it had been scripted by Tennessee Williams with parts for Greta Garbo and Mae West. Its indiscipline would be the despair of the

Sunday garden writers. No plantsman's garden (though there's a wide range of species), it bursts out like a big girl's blouse in a lush and vulgar profusion of colour.

Not for some time, however, was I to get rid of the huge quantity of weed seed — and its progeny — that had been dumped over the years next to the barn door to the granary. "Well, you know what they say?" said my friend Allen Paterson, then director of the Royal Botanical Gardens (RBG) in Hamilton, cheerfully: "One year's seeding, nine years' weeding. I reckon you have about two hundred years' here."

What I also had were some pleasant surprises. A suggestion by "Granny" that he clear out what looked an impossible dump underneath some old apples to the east of the Great Garden led to the discovery that the site was quite flat and had, in fact (I later discovered from some of my great-aunt's tapes), been the site of the first barn. And so "Barn Lawn" (now also hedged by white pines), and the first stage of the eastern vista from the Great Garden, were born.

Without our consciously setting about to do so, the overall plan began to acquire those twin aspects of surprise and variety that were also the hallmark of the early eighteenth-century landscape. Writing to Lord Burlington in 1731, Pope translated Horace to come up with a recipe that still remains true:

> *He gains all points, who pleasingly confounds,*
> *Surprizes, varies, and conceals the Bounds.*

So Barn Lawn, extending the garden eastward through a
"room" of grass, did what another great garden designer,
Reginald Blomfield, also recommended. It took the architecture of the house gradually out into the landscape and
softened the abruptness of the geometry of the overall plan.

Height in the Great Garden was to be achieved with
four tall Japanese crab-apples for definition, one in the centre of each quadrant. There were also variations in level in
the Great Garden: not great ones, but enough to give a
sense of different spaces and hidden places. The relish for
such things was brought into English gardens by the man
who had most to do with introducing Italian taste, James I's
ambassador to Venice, Sir Henry Wotton. In *The Elements of
Architecture* (1624), he noted that the difference between
buildings and gardens was that, whereas the former "should
bee *regular*, so Gardens should bee *irregular*, or at least cast
into a very wilde *Regularitie*." From his experience of the
terraced gardens of the Veneto, he saw that what was beautiful about the gardens of the Countess of Bedford at Moor
Park was that one could see the whole plan of it, but
"rather in a delightfull confusion, than with any plain dis-
tinction of the pieces". And he noticed that this was chiefly
achieved by differences in elevation, or what he called
"several *mountings* and *valings*". Eight years after I began the
Great Garden, Sir Henry finally got his memorial in
Stonyground. The steps leading west from the Great Garden
go first to the hedge-on-sticks walk, and then down next
to the rose garden. Just where the difference in elevation is

greatest, carved in the steps is the text: "Several *mountings* and *valings*".

Into the Great Garden went the (very good) topsoil from the site of the hedge-on-sticks walk: not the first of the many labours undertaken for me by my cousin Campbell and his redoubtable John Deere tractor. John Deere should do a commercial showing how useful that tractor is as a gardening tool. Some future archaeologist will discover that the six-foot width of many of the walks and beds here coincides with the "bucket" on that tractor: a bucket that had already (during my absence in the previous autumn) made a new perennial border near the house — double-digging and manuring it in one fell swoop. As I write this, he has just used it to make the ha-ha by the barn. But I am running ahead of myself.

Campbell's interest in the garden has traced an interesting trajectory. At least as sceptical initially as others in the family and neighbourhood, he has moved through curiosity and bemusement to enthusiasm and major contribution, including suggestions of material and design. As we share the name "Campbell" (the name of our grandmother's family that lived here), it may be that he feels something of what I do for the place. But he wears his feelings and commitments more inwardly than I do.

My floral loves and hates are aired more openly, though the latter are always stronger among gardeners. I was pleased to discover that the Edwardian gardener E.A. Bowles disliked hybridized dahlias as much as I do. When

I was at Cambridge a friend's bedmaker in the college put her back out hanging her plastic flowers up to dry. It seemed to me one of the proofs of the existence of God. I have always thought of dahlias as nature's answer to plastic flowers: the ultimate dead end of flower-arranging. The splendid cartoonist Glen Baxter seems to agree with Bowles and me. One of his cartoons shows a cowboy taking aim at a particularly gaudy specimen, with the caption: "Zeke had a way with dahlias."

Bowles didn't think much of Mediterranean marigolds either, and nor do I, though I've been persuaded by organicists to use them occasionally in the *potager* to ward off insect pests. Only recently, with the advent of the lovely *Celosia spicata*, have I been reconciled to that species too, though I still find their dwarf cousins (the appropriately named "kewpie") the ugly feather-dusters of the garden. The same goes for the strident red salvia, though the pale blue *Salvia patens* is one of the gardener's treasures. (Indeed, it was the municipal-gardener horrors of ageratum and red salvia and marigolds that led me that year to propose to my college in Toronto that I be allowed to replant one of the beds there with a combination of pink and white autumnal perennials to complement the grey stone of the buildings.)

But there are the loves too: the great blowsy lilies of July that fill the evening air with a perfume that is (almost) enough to make the gardener forget all disasters and disappointments. Some authors think that the "lilies of the field" of the New Testament must have been tulips, but much as I like tulips I cannot believe that lilies are not what was meant. Especially the Turk's-caps hanging down like golden lamps in the evening air. And the poppies, too, that the poet laureate Ted Hughes has described so well in the line: "Her big, lewd, bold eye, in its sooty lashes."

Above all, the Great Garden is a place to sit in the evening, among these scents and lushnesses, sometimes with friends and talk and music; sometimes alone with the late hummingbirds and the early moths. "Restfulness," said Sir George Sitwell, "is the prevailing note of an old garden." So, I would like to think, it is becoming at Stonyground, where even the distantly clanking repair shop becomes metamorphosed into the village smithy.

At Stonyground the prevailing northwest wind is the gardener's enemy. In a garden hedged by pines — an idea that I had discovered at the RBG in Hamilton — the south-facing barn wall (eighty feet high) would eventually create a micro-climate. Adjacent to it, at the southern end (nearest the house), would be an oval garden with a little recirculating fountain in a buried sewer tile: a black garden as a sort of joke on the fashion for white gardens, one of which would in fact be next to it, outside beyond the hedge.

The original plan shows the fountain as part of a recirculating water system connected by a "rill" to a pond at the centre of the garden. But it has taken years of thought and advice to figure out how to make a water channel that will not break up in the sub-zero winter weather. And only now does it seem likely that that literal pipe-dream can be realized: a fused plastic (pvc) trough concealed with over-lapping flagstones.

Some of the Great Garden was planted that summer, though July was late for it. I had removed to the Great Garden what plants remained of an old border, the original flower garden made by my great-grandmother. That border had been too far from the house to be appreciated and, in any case, by the time I arrived, much of it had been over-run by couch grass (the worst of weeds here) and burdocks that another cousin had found so indistinguishable from hollyhocks that at one time he had murdered both.

Where did the rest of the flowers come from? Some of them were gifts, divisions from friends and relatives and neighbours. And for some of them I had gone farther afield — to Gerry Brickman's extensive perennial nursery at Wartburg, for example, and even so far away as nurseries in Toronto. Much of this was to be experiment and chance, the luck of the draw in spite of what the zone maps might say. Some things that ought not to have prospered have. Heather, for example, which needs snow cover to endure our winters, will thrive at Stonyground when it will not survive in the treacherous mildness of the RBG in Hamilton. But I have never had any luck with yuccas, though they will grow cheerfully only a few miles south of my garden.

Some iris went in at that time, but they've since come out, to fight it out in another bed with the equally invasive day lilies. Erigeron and pink delphiniums, some tulips, pulmonaria, astilbe and cranesbill, bergenia and pinks, and the little pink lamium for edging: those for openers in the pink garden, followed by peonies and lupines and the odd patch of sweet rocket. Later, the pink veronica and the lavatera and malvas, and finally, the various pinks of the phloxes and the sturdy chelones taking one into autumn, accompanied by *Sedum spectabile.*

And so in all the quadrants, some of them more spectacular at one time than another, as if the sun were coming and going in different parts of the garden at different times. When the pink is least spectacular, the orange quadrant is ablaze with day lilies and lilies, red-hot pokers, wallflowers and geum. Later, when its helianthus and helenium take over, it is the turn of the red quadrant to look most special: the towering dark red of the hollyhocks behind a scrim of lychnis and red achillea and the late red tiger lilies.

None of this happened all at once, and there has been much moving of things about over the years as colours proved untrue and heights unsatisfactory. Ground covers like spurge and artemisia, which seemed a great idea in the first place, have had to be curbed from strangling everything else. And there are always newcomers to be accommodated: some Russian sunflowers next to the barn in the orange quadrant, or a foxtail lily to perk up the corner of the yellow.

During that summer I was busy at work on the long perennial border that had been made near the house the previous autumn. That border was also planted according to

Gertrude Jekyll's dictates, in a colour perspective that attempted to keep some things in each colour in flower throughout the summer. What a business it was — and remains! — trying to outguess what will sport back to the original colour or to determine what will bloom when in semi-shade as opposed to full sun! Everything is experiment for the true gardener, even for a gardener like the Duchess of Beaufort in the seventeenth century who had a host of sub-gardeners at her command. Someone — probably the Queen's gardener, Leonard Plukenet — had sent her yellow loosestrife (*Lysimachia*), that hardy yellow-spiked charmer of early summer. "Lysimachia, the pritty plant that blows [blooms] all summer," he had written. The duchess had found otherwise; in her hand, next to Plukenet's entry, is the word "false".

The preparation of the hedge-on-sticks site was the last thing to be done that year. Stripped of its topsoil, it was filled with "pit-run" (the lowest form of gravel) and topped with proper gravel, and then stone-dust, so that it sloped gently up towards the barn at the northern end. (Stone-dust is a finely ground powdery gravel that packs down well into walks and, although nothing will eliminate weeds altogether, it provides a fairly effective way of dealing with them.) Not to be planted until the following spring, the hedge-on-sticks was the "fudge" in the whole plan, the place where the fact that nothing was square to anything else could be concealed by cunning planting on the edges.

Was that the first year for cider? I wonder. Certainly it was not long until I recognized that my three old apple trees — Cortlands and Snows — provided far more fruit than I could use. And "use" meant (and means) "use there and then . . . or freeze" — for these wonderful old apples are not good "keepers". They have none of the tasteless and well-preserved good looks of the things called apples that fill our supermarkets. Cider it was — and fertilizer bags filled to the brim with sometimes fairly mongrel apples — all went off to the local cider mill at Carlsruhe. There the apples rattle up a washing conveyor to the press, and dark real apple juice (so different from that watery anaemic stuff) pours like honey from the folded cloths of the press. This was to become a September ritual — or at least every other year, as these old trees bear heavily only biennially: another reason for their going out of fashion.

It must have been at this point that I began to see clearly what was being achieved in the gardens . . . or at any rate, to see beyond the messy chaos with which I began. Odd the moment (or is it a moment?) at which one begins to realize that the whole thing is more than a pipe-dream. Perhaps it comes with the first few friends who say, "Oh, now I see what this is all about"— and not just in a despairing tone of voice. It was to be some time before anyone locally took it all seriously, though. Most of them — even my cousins — could not imagine such a project as anything other than a potentially money-making operation.

By the end of the summer of 1986, most of the original plan of the gardens, first drafted a year earlier, had been put in place. But gardens are more than plans, and in any case, one puts one plan into place only in order to see that there are others waiting in the wings. And so it has gone on. But I know that at the end of that season I stood in the garden, thinking of the scrappy little trees one can see in the photographs of the gardens of Lawrence Johnston's Hidcote in its early years, and knowing that something had at last begun to be accomplished at Stonyground. The scrappy little trees already meant that the foundations had been laid.

CHAPTER 4

THE BONES GO IN

THE HEDGE-ON-STICKS

Bonfires and chain-saws: in the spring of 1987 we cut down eight trees near the house to let the light in. And then that first whiff of March, something primitive stirring, like what Mole smells in *The Wind in the Willows:* shovels and house (or garden) cleaning. O leaves! Well you do not have old maples without lots of them, and you do not have good compost without raking them up. That was one of the things I learned about as a kid — compost heaps: the one hidden by shrubbery in the back corner of the house in North Toronto, always being added to and turned over.

Even Eden, as Milton described it, had a compost yard. The poet refers to its "garden mould". But compost is not the mystique that the radio garden experts want to make it: a matter for daily attention with nail scissors and special bins. Most of what comes out of the garden over the season will break down on its own. You need some "wormy circumstance" to get it going and to keep it at work through the long days of grass clippings, but what are manure piles (and neighbouring farms) for? I laugh every spring at the bags of "bovine fertilizer" in the local supermarket in town, when the farms are steaming with heaps of it, often for the asking. Yes, it smells, but if you don't like that sort of smell, you're probably no real gardener. Contemplating the rotting lion and the hive of bees in his belly, the prophet said: "Out of the strong came forth sweetness." It's a good motto for more than the makers of Tate and Lyle's sugar syrup!

If you're lucky, you'll be near a horse farm. Horse manure has the advantage over cow in that, whereas the cow's many stomachs do not destroy all of the weed seeds that she eats, the horse's single stomach does. At worst your compost heap will need some urea (the name bespeaks its origin) from a farm-supply store. Cheap, effective, and clean, and with a couple of handfuls now and then, a bag will last the summer. I have never had one of those fancy turning poles or any of the other expensive garden-store gizmos. "Oh, Mrs. Verey," said some French women once to the owner of Barnsley, "how do you have such large perennials?" "Beaucoup de leaf-mould" was Rosemary's reply.

Well, you'll have to fuss with it if you want to compost everything. If you want to add shrub- and tree-trimmings, you'll need to burn them, as they take forever to rot and simply annoy you when you're trying to use the compost. And there are some weeds (couch grass, lamb's-quarters and pigweed, for example) that it is folly to put straight into the compost heap unless you fancy weeding on a big scale. I have a yard for such weeds on the site of the old henhouse. The yard is hedged and pretty well invisible, and in it are an incinerator and two concrete-block compost bins with a heavy metal grid near the bottom. They are for the compost that needs "finessing", and behind the yard is the manure pile, annually renewed.

One thing that also needs finessing is apples: I mean the rotten falls that clutter any lawn or garden which has the good fortune to have old apple trees near it. There is no spraying apple trees forty feet tall. That's part of the reason why standard-size apple trees went out of fashion. But who wants the bother and expense of spraying anyway? The way to deal with apple-worm is to keep the falls away from under the trees . . . as the pigs or cattle used to do in the old days. So into these composters the wormy and rotten apples go, along with lots of woodash from the stoves and the incinerator over the fall and winter. This is how I have good compost.

Some of it goes out in the spring, around the new plantings, perhaps with a little bone or blood meal mixed in. Most of it, though, goes out in August, when the garden slows down and one can get on with the other jobs that need also to be done but have not been squeaking so loudly: around favourite roses or to make up new beds.

In the spring of 1987, as in the three previous Marchs, we started as early as the frost was out of the ground to dig and replant the maples that would make the landscape avenues. Always (it seemed) in the streaming rain — like bulb-planting later, and with the desperation of knowing that you had only a limited time to do it ... and a limited number of years to see them grow up!

And this was also the year for planting the hedge-on-sticks: about eighty littleleaf lindens tenderly nurtured in the topsoil that we had put on the edge of the inhospitable gravel and "pit-run" of the walk constructed the previous year. Either the North American native hornbeam or the introduced species, littleleaf linden, would do, but in the end it was the latter, for hornbeam is only marginally hardy here, and it is very expensive. And the lindens have the advantage of their heady scent in June.

It's difficult, this business of local versus exotic. The "patriots of horticulture", as the early gardeners of the eighteenth century called themselves, spent much of their time arguing about whether Virgil approved or disapproved of exotics. On the one hand, he seemed to stress growing things that prospered where you were and, on the other, to encourage experimentation with the whole range of botany. Well, that's just where any sensible gardener is too. I have a rule of thumb with "exotics": the death of a specimen on a first try may be a fluke; on the second, it's not.

I've (expensively) tried tulip-trees and (less expensively) redbud, which (in spite of its name — *Cercis canadensis*) seems not to want to flourish in its home and native land. I know whereof I speak, though I have recently been tempted to folly again by a local nurseryman who assures me that more mature specimens will survive. Like *Magnolia stellata*, he claims, they will be fastigiate (shrubby), not arboreal (tree-like), but they will survive. I've planted one of each in a new garden near the house. We'll see.

Rhododendrons are a moot point. They *will* grow this far north (they grow in the Himalayas, after all), but their love of acid soil means that the only suitable place for them here is down under the pines, by the lake. One of them still survives there, though its North American cousins, mountain laurel, turned up their precious toes.

So one goes on, year after year, trying to push at the edges of things, planting things that the experts say won't grow and waiting to see. Sometimes luck is with you. On the east side of the house, in the most protected bed, out of reach of the prevailing northwest wind, there are hellebores growing: the Christmas and the Lenten rose, as they are sometimes called, though here they bloom at the same time. And one of the great pleasures is in passing cuttings on to local gardening friends, creating another local flora.

"Is this hardy with you?" the visiting English garden-ladies are fond of asking, when they're not observing, "You have no cedars in Canada." (It's true, we don't; our cedars are *Thuja* species, but it's difficult not to feel irked by the condescension, or to feel one ought to take a leaf from their book.) "Why is it," one of them said to me, "that you did not make an authentically Canadian garden instead of an English one?" "Do you mean the sort of 'authentically

English garden' that the ancient Celts made?" I asked.

In his play *Arcadia*, Tom Stoppard puts his finger on the absurdity of this kind of proprietorial gardening. "Ah," says one of the characters about the eighteenth-century landscapes of Capability Brown, "the real England."

> *You can stop being silly now, Bernard [says Hannah, the garden historian]. English landscape was invented by gardeners imitating foreign painters who were evoking classical authors. The whole thing was brought home in the luggage from the grand tour.*

But what might an "authentically Canadian garden" be (once one's got past the initial absurdity of one garden style representing a country that's larger than Europe)? Whatever I am doing at Stonyground can hardly be the same as the tidy perfections of city gardens, but it has the advantage of a palette of large plants that would look absurdly overgrown in those gardens. Sometimes it is a matter of experimenting with local plants to see whether they prosper companionably. There are always surprises in that department. My mother's favourite wild flower was the showy lady's slipper, but when I planted some of those rare beauties in a damp grove that I thought they would like, they turned up their toes. And yet one has prospered in a new dry bed near the house. And "blue devil" (viper's bugloss, another of her favourites) will grow self-seeded in the gravelly barnyard, but it will not prosper in the border.

"How do you get such big plants in your climate?" asked a woman recently at a meeting of the Friends of the Oxford Botanic Garden, where I was giving a talk. "They grow quickly," I said. So do the weeds: just like Jack's beanstalk. First the dandelions in the lawn kept cut early to stop them seeding into the beds, and then in the beds themselves: marsh mallow and sheep sorrel (called "red dock" here) with their ferocious tap roots (so resistant to the worst winter), and then the Medusa roots of couch grass and sow thistle, their rhizomes snaking away and always breaking off so that new plants can form. I do not generally use herbicides on the beds, but on the walks there is no keeping ahead of the perpetual seeding-in of weeds in the prevailing northwest wind without "Roundup" or some such systemic herbicide that is not a residual.

So, the wild flowers were brought home to England and the weeds were exported. They're our legacy of empire. (Scarcely a grass is growing east of the Mississippi that was there when Columbus landed, says Alfred Crosby, the author of *Ecological Imperialism*.) Each spring begins with war, mostly against English weeds. Couch grass, plantain, Canada thistle, burdock, red dock, shepherd's purse, purslane — the list goes on and on.

After one has weeded for a year or two, one becomes convinced that there is such a thing as plant intelligence. Why is it that the leaves of red dock look so like the early radicchios, and how does Queen Anne's lace know that its feathery fronds will be indistinguishable among the carrots?

Even some of the grasses contrive to look like young onions.

But spring is not only about weeding, or even replacing plants. Almost at once there is the business of tending and tying up and getting the supporting baskets around the peonies in the week or so (it seems) between their appearance and their being too large to deal with. But first, even before any of that is possible, comes the old clump of snowdrops (planted long before my time) by the honeysuckle at the bottom of the lawn. There they are, almost invisible winged messengers of what is to come: untouchable, not to be picked, the Gypsies believe, lest nothing else blossom that year. And then, gradually, the aconites that I have added, and bit by bit all those little under-lawn bulbs that give the gardener a partial respite from lawn-mowing: blue and white scillas; *Pulchella violacea*; and the leaves of the late-flowering narcissus, whose blooms come last. In the beds the various tulips, from the early *Kaufmanniana* to the late Darwins, and with the earliest, the wonderful lush blossoms of the hellebores.

O bulbs! One of the gardener's curses is the colour-blindness of suppliers: orange tulips that turn out to be red, or "apricot" Jacob's ladder that comes out pink. The colour-graded plan of the Great Garden's four quadrants is (or was) that, as you approached the barn (its northern termination), the colour perspective would grow darker in palette and so lengthen the effect in the same way as the gradually tapering main walk. But that depends on some degree of confidence about what you are buying from the nursery. Linnaeus's whole system of botanical nomenclature arose partly so that gardeners could be sure they were not ordering the same plant twice under different names. Some consistency in what nurserymen consider to be orange or pink would be a help too.

I've never been entirely happy with the bulbs in the Great Garden. Perhaps they look better in rectangular borders than in essentially square beds. And certainly they cannot be naturalized — not even the wild species tulips — in the way that the suppliers cheerfully advertise. Well, not naturalized in this nature anyway, where the dear little rodents go after them underground and the groundhogs wait for their spring salad of the first nice tulip buds.

What goes out into the landscape — into the walks round and through the working farm that were my original idea for this place? Well, not much for the first few years as I became increasingly distracted by the gardens around the house. Eventually, however, I was to plant about ten thousand (mostly Darwin) tulips in the avenue to the woods: a colour perspective from orange near the house to black at the woods. But that was several years off and took several autumns' planting, often during the first snowstorm of October.

And in any case it was only partially successful. Most hybridized tulips will recur for several years in flowerbeds, but they are not up to dealing with the weedy nature of a farm lane. The exception seems to be the cardinal reds that

The main avenue to the woods showing the tulips planted next to the old fencerow

are closest to the species tulip. Brashly they return from year to year, so I suppose I shall have to make do with half a mile of scarlet as a spring flourish. Perhaps I should have been content with the bloodroot and dog-tooth violets that seem to know how to hold their own there, but I was determined to see how much of Southcote's idea of rifling the garden for the hedgerows would work.

It's worked much better in another avenue across the farm that I was not to make until 1990. There, I've used daffodils between the trees that line the walk, and even the little creatures know that daffodils are poisonous. Daffodils are also great spreaders. But one needs to keep the grass cut last thing in the autumn to make sure that the blooms show to advantage in spring . . . and the grass in the walk cut early to prevent the daffodils having to compete with the flashy sunny-side-up of the dandelions. Mowing on that scale is another story, however.

But 1987 was long before any of that kind of planting. It was the spring to finish planting the Great Garden properly, with its great colour range, chosen to spread as long as possible from early spring to late autumn. In went curiosities like *Rheum palmatum*, with its strange plume of pink, and the first of the alliums, and echinops and eryngium, the first of an increasing number of thistles that are manageable in the garden.

One of the things I had learned from Allen Paterson was to get over the zone-itis of most Canadian (or Ontario) gardeners: nothing before the 24th of May and nothing after Labour Day. Never, I think, has my cousin Campbell been so scandalized as by my offering him four vegetables fresh from the garden at the end of November!

So, much digging and manuring and weeding, in what seemed an endless round. This was to be the first year that I had more than friends to help: a hired man–turned–weeder who nonetheless found it all a bit overwhelming and left within a month. Tree-planting too, not just continuing to line the avenues with transplanted maples, but the Great Garden with seedling white pines. Ultimately this would form a six-foot hedge, the sort of "hedge of feathers" that I had seen made with white pine in the RBG's arboretum. With the south-facing eighty-foot-high wall of the barn, it would create a micro-climate that would extend the growing year and make plants possible that were not supposedly hardy here. Barn Lawn was hedged with pines too, and the beginning of an outer shelterbelt of pines and spruces was made, out beyond the barn — to break the prevailing northwest wind.

By now the garden was beginning to be known, and the problem of how to identify the place for visitors was a real one. The farm had had a postbox by the road, but it had long ago been the victim of a snowplough and been tucked away in the barn with the "Century Farm" sign and what was left of the old implements. Since a mailbox spewing out a week or two's worth of circulars was a sure sign of absence, I had got a post-office box in town in any case. The solution? Well, Campbell had found a handsome granite boulder, and I persuaded the somewhat reluctant monument mason from town to haul it away to his shop and to carve "Stonyground" into it. I'm no longer entirely happy with its typeface (it looks a bit as if "lies here" should follow), but its arrival that spring was a great moment: champagne for the workers at least, with a little for the stone.

I spent most of the rest of that summer plotting: making apricot espaliers on the barn and planting bittersweet and trumpet vine to climb up through them on to the grey wood of the barn walls . . . imagining a new pump-house, a possible terrace by the barn, a seat on its garden side. These are the dreams that get you through the drear of autumn clean-up: the leaves that never seem to stop falling and the seeming acres of dead perennials to be cut back, the planting pots to be turned over or put away. But autumn is when the landscape's garden also comes into its own: drifts of wild asters (or Michaelmas daisies) in all sorts of colours and textures; the handsome drying heads of teasel and milkweed and money plant; and behind it all, as the season drifts into October, the great flamey backdrop of the hardwood maples.

Part of the Great Garden in spring

CHAPTER 5

Mixing the Beautiful
with the Useful

The Pump-house

The next year, 1988, was to be chiefly the year of the pump-house. City-dwellers are continually astonished that the farm is not on a water main, as a farm might be in England. Here, we have a well, down to the largest underground river in southern Ontario. Or so says my geological neighbour Sid Timms, who has given up the migraine of a high-school classroom for a congenial life of antique-selling. (It was Sid who told me what to do with my walnut trees too, but more on that later.) That "river" has recently been rediscovered by an underwater-survey team in their pocket submarine. It leaves Georgian Bay, on one side of the Bruce Peninsula, over an underwater waterfall (how do such things work?) before flowing under the limestone bedrock of the county to empty into Lake Huron.

What an extraordinary thing a well is, and how constant a reminder of the fragility of the ecosystem. If the town pumps too much water, my neighbours' wells go dry. (Mine is 130 feet deep, and therefore immune to such vagaries.) If someone somewhere is dumping atomic waste into underground reservoirs or using a dangerous herbicide, it will find its way into the subterranean water reserves. And yet how wonderful it is to drink water that does not taste of last week's bleach, as city water does!

But the operation of a well and its pump is an almost Masonic mystery. Its maintenance and repair require someone who knows about electricity, plumbing, and the ritual of foot-valves, if one is not to be left literally high and dry by a bunch of different repairmen, each blaming the others for its failure.

Fortunately there was, and is, such a man — Howard Whitehead, who had grown up two farms away and gone on to become an electrician, a plumber, and a "well-man": a man who knew the local wells as intimately as a farmer knows his fields. Who else to get to deal with all the mechanics of the pump-house? — the sort of person who would come out in the evening to dig the pipes down deeper in newly laid concrete because the contractors (to his disgust) had raised them above frost level in setting the forms. Slightly lame from a roof-fall (is anyone in the country uninjured?), he nonetheless can clamber down to a pump, work in the confined space of its dry-well, and come up with the whole operation ticking over again, even on a sub-zero day, when it seems that the machinery may have packed up until next spring.

That spring we demolished the old pump-house: another insulbrick charmer that, when I was a child in the days before electricity here, had contained the marvel of the neighbourhood. This was a gasoline-driven pump that was fired up once or twice a day to raise the pressure in the big tank in the cellar of the house, and so supply both house and barn. A big gauge by the sink in the old kitchen told when the pressure was sufficient. Long since replaced with what turned out to be an inadequate electric pump, its original housings were still there, as well as several decades' walnut shells deposited over long winters by industrious red squirrels. Fortunately (I guess) they still keep the black ones at bay, screaming their mad Beatrix Potter impertinences from the century-old Norway spruces, and hiding walnuts in every corner of the barn that they have made their condo.

The barn is another story. Dominating the top of the hill like a cathedral, its essentially medieval structure (most of it put together without nails) is both terrifying and exhilarating to me. The exhilaration is in its vast spaces and magnificent beams: and is activated in part by my not-quite-suppressed recollection of having had to be rescued by my uncle at the age of five from a vertigo terror that would not let me climb down again from a hay loft. But it is a beautiful building, a structure not unlike great medieval timber-frame houses: houses like the two that Christopher

Lloyd's father put together at the centre of his magnificent garden, Great Dixter.

And there is also a great beauty, even in the names of the barn's parts, names forgotten by all but countrymen like my cousin: its gerts and its purlins, words for beams that have long disappeared from common use. Recently I heard Salman Rushdie lamenting the loss of the polyglot: a world of words as lush as the Amazonian rain forest being swept aside by a kind of burger-speak. Here, still thriving at the margins, those old words keep a weedy and lively existence: "whippletree", "coulter", and "mould-board" for implement parts; "freemartin" for sterile twin calves or "beestings" for the cow's first milk; and fields still measured in rods.

This barn was built in 1870, and pulled apart in 1917 to expand it by an extra third. In the middle, the beams are machine-milled; on the sides, one can still see the marks of the hand-hewn axe and the great pegs put into holes made with a two-man drill. Up, up it soars, about eighty feet from the threshing floor, through this elaborate geometry. My terror now is not in remembering childhood vertigo but in recognizing that here is a cathedral that I have to keep up: roofs to repair, foundations to rebuild.

What is odd (as with so many things in the country) is how ignorant many people in the local towns are of all this life of the country: its names, its equipment, its manner of life. Recently, when my half-feral barn cat ran amok and gave me a painful bite, the local medical authorities told

Looking from the house towards the Great Garden and the barn past the pump-house; in the foreground the Pope inscription in the walk

me that I had to confine the cat in the barn for ten days to observe it for rabies. Confine a cat in a barn like this, designed to be open to the wind so that its hay would ventilate? I couldn't help wondering where these people had been living. Plainly their lives did not depend on the fields, nor did their water come from wells!

The pump-house had long outlived itself, though, and down it came. Once reroofed by my great-aunt when she was in her eighties, the pump-house unravelled a mystery in its demolition. The International Plowing Match had been held on my cousins' nearby farm in the early 1970s. A hundred-acre trade show, in effect, it was held again last year on the same site, providing the usual rag-bag of politicians and salesmen with a platform to make their pitches. After the previous match, however, the big (plywood) sign announcing the event had mysteriously disappeared overnight. This was at a time when one of my uncles was farming Stonyground, and it was he (it turned out) who had "cabbaged" it (one of my great-aunt's favourite words) to reroof the pump-house . . . where we found it.

Into the gravel-pit bonfire went the pump-house (minus the plywood) so that new footings could be poured and a new structure built. Not that this had been an effortless process to arrange. The man who had been recommended to me for the job took one look at Ron's gothic plans and turned the whole thing over to his brother's building firm. The problem was the bell-canted roof that we wanted, but fortunately Jim Spitzig and his partner, Ray Ernewein,

were more lithe of mind and body than Ray's brother. And
so the pump-house, a sort of "quotation" from the pavil-
ions at Hidcote in Gloucestershire, was built, though in
wood, not brick.

Well, perhaps not quite so easily as that sounds, and
seems in my retrospective mind. Things are rarely as one
remembers them. Why does learning to drive (and getting
a truck) that summer now seem so commonplace when I
know that the whole process was one of farce mixed with
terror? "What is material to this diary?" I find myself having written that summer on the day when I discovered that
I was HIV-negative. Could I have gone on with all this —
would I? — if the result had been otherwise?

"This book looks like a hyper-text," said a writer friend
who picked up the first few pages of the first draft. "Not
hyper-text but 'intra-text'," I said. There is no one text in
its writing, any more than in the making of the garden
itself; all the texts interweave with one another. Somewhere
in the centre of this book is the chronology of it all, but the
structure of the book as a whole is almost as obscure as the
origin of the spider's web. Many texts are here — cultural,
personal, historical, botanical — all of them leaking into the
discourse of one another and creating something that even
I will not understand, probably, until years from now . . .
if then.

It took most of the summer for the builders to come,
though once they did they worked very quickly and ended
up constructing the Rousham seat by the barn too. A roofed

enclosure with a seat, it was slightly larger than its original, thereby allowing its bulk to compete with the even greater mass of the barn. And it must be congruent too, for city-slickers who know nothing of barns often imagine it might have been the original barn entrance. No, it is a place to sit and contemplate and to look down the two-hundred-foot walk to the woods across the road: a vista of flowerbeds and trees, though seldom (once summer comes) without our friend the mosquito. No amount of citronella geraniums seems ever to keep *them* away.

Part of that vista includes the new pump-house. Surrounded with a delicate verandah and roofed with the local white-cedar shingles, it is a handsome thing painted grey and white by yet another friend who is as fond of painting as I am not: "The Pump Room", as my unkind friends call it, ridiculing its pretensions. But nothing can beat local candour. "Like your shed," said the kid across the road. And it's not just the kids. When I had to get the property evaluated recently, I found the pump-house described as "utility shed". Well, I suppose it is. Operation Central for the garden, it stands almost in the middle, dispensing tools and hoses and looking rather like a lady of quality being gracious to those who are certainly her inferiors.

The pump-house is topped by a finial made by one of the local patriarchs, Herb Miller. Herb is the effective founder of the Welbeck Sawmill over in Bentinck Township, about thirty miles away, in Grey County. Famous for its water-driven shingle mill (the source of the shingles for the pump-house), it also boasts the hardware store of every carpenter's dreams: walls of different-sized English chisels, Swedish benches one would happily use as desks, barrels of square nails, and a staff who know exactly what you're looking for and where it is, or even where else you might find it.

Most famous for founding the Durham Wood Show (an annual display of the work of local cabinet-makers and the tools of their trade), Herb must now be in his eighties, but he carries on like someone half that age. I thought I had seen finials at Welbeck — it's the sort of place where you could believe you'd seen anything — and I asked him about it. "Oh, no," he said, "you can't get one of them ready-made. I'll make you one, though, but I can't do it right away. I've got the Wood Show next week." Three days later, the finial was ready.

How odd such things are in the country! Either you get that sort of quiet professionalism or you get a ham-fisted "that'll do": a steel roof put on, not with screws, but with nails that pop in the sub-zero winters and leave your barn prey to high winds, or a plastic eavestrough that *looks* like the real thing until you lean your ladder against it and find it has cracked in two. Fortunately, most of my experience has been of the quiet professionals, and often from people like Howard Whitehead who can turn their hand to more than one thing.

One of the casualties in all this pump-house business was the water supply to the barn, where I had noticed what seemed an active spring when I first came. It turned out to be the water main to the barn, which had ultimately to be turned off at the well: no great loss then as I had no intention of keeping cattle. But I realize, now that the gardens have expanded and proliferated, that another water source closer to them would have been useful.

The pump-house was built, later to be complemented by a stone inscription suggested by a friend, George Clarke, the historian of the greatest of the eighteenth-century English gardens, Stowe. Horace was what George suggested — the famous quotation from his *Art of Poetry* about the man winning the day who mixes the beautiful with the useful. George thought it might go on the pump-house itself, but the building is too delicate for that, even for an eavestrough. However, for just that reason I had surrounded it with flagstones to prevent erosion, and the flagstones across the front proved just the right number, one for each word: *"Omne tulit punctum qui miscuit utile dulci."*

That inscription in a handsome roman type was one of the early ones to be carved by a new discovery: a stone-carver suggested to me by the one in Walkerton, who plainly thought Stonyground too zany to deal with. Tobey Soper has come to be a good friend: a fifth-generation stone-carver, whose ancestors worked on Salisbury Cathedral and the Houses of Parliament at Westminster. In 1987 he began with another boulder, a deltoid monster brought up (with great effort) by the 150-horsepower tractor from the back of the farm, where it must have been removed from a field long ago by horses.

The deltoid was to be "delta", a "D" for "Diana"— "suitable for country situations", as one seventeenth-century writer put it. And on it Tobey carved a Greek bow that he found in one of his own reference books. It was the first mythologizing here, but not the last, and it stands on guard on the far side of Barn Lawn, where the fields begin. There, on the line of the cross-access in the Great Garden, that symbolic stone stands now (seven years later) at the beginning of the transverse avenue, lined with its rows of pyramidal cedars and leading eventually to a temple more than six hundred feet away.

Probably these inscriptions seem the most bewildering (and perhaps infuriating) aspect of the garden to most visitors. Their largely private significance (they're primarily for my enjoyment) seems exclusive to those who aren't in the know, but then the same would be true of a hockey game to a Tibetan. The simplest explanation is that they're my writing back into the landscape the texts that arose from it and that, in turn, inspired me in the first place.

Sometimes the references are so private that only one friend would "get" the joke. That year was the three-hundredth anniversary of the accession of the Dutch king William III to the English throne. It seemed to call for a Dutch moment in the garden, and so (partly in homage also to a Dutch garden-historian friend) one of the berms was planted with orange tulips. In Bruce County that's something of a double joke, for the old orange day lilies that grow on every roadside now were often referred to in the past as "Twelfth of July Lilies" as if they blossomed in honour of William III's victory over the Catholic Irish at the Battle of the Boyne.

That past was in the days of the Protestant Ascendancy, when the loyalty of Catholics was suspect and the Orange Day parade was the great event of the year. Halfway between Toronto and Stonyground, Orangeville commemorates in its name a culture of what Matthew Arnold called "the Protestantism of the Protestant Religion". Dourness and bombazine and grim Sundays: "Well, you won't get out of that," said my grandmother cheerfully to my father on his wedding day. Professor Goldwin Smith, Arnold wrote, must have had abundant experience of all this in the long winter evenings in Toronto. How much more so in the country, where a decision in the local Presbyterian church to replace cantors with an organ was greeted with cries of "Popery!"

The nearest village to my farm is called Chepstow. That is not the name the Irish Catholic villagers wanted to give it. "Emmet" was their choice, after Robert Emmet, who led the Irish rising against the English in 1803. The government said that the village was to be named "Chepstow", after the first English earl to subdue the Irish. That was the old Ontario.

And yet here, where Catholic Irish and Germans worked in the fields alongside Protestant Scots and Irish, there was rarely any personal hostility. Only at threshings, where a double cuisine of meat and fish had to be provided on

Fridays, was there any sense of "apartheid". One great-aunt who had forgotten to make the usual provision for fish was heard to observe that the Catholics could "eat meat or do the other thing". And to the men, it was evidence of a Protestant God that the Catholics who had waited for the Catholic threshing-machine had their harvest rained on.

Now there is a different demography, and it is what the English would call the "offcomers" who are suspect: the painters and sculptors and potters and weavers who have found in this landscape the right refuge. Some of them have made the county famous, but the old-timers will be the last to know . . . or care. So far as I know, Walkerton has only once appeared in what might be called "world litera-ture": a short story called "Wigtime" by Alice Munro. She has listened to these local voices and set them down unforget-tably, but the local high school does not even have all of her novels in the library, and even Wingham, her home town, has no plaque or monument to her existence.

Another Allen Paterson suggestion was put in place that summer: the main walk connecting the Great Garden to the house in a way which that garden demanded. And it also made sense of the previous placing of the new peren-nial border closer to the house. Yet another labour of the John Deere tractor, the walk is six feet wide and terminates at the northern end, by the barn. At the south, it looks across the new orchard on the hill below the house and across to the woods beyond, "calling in" the country round about.

Looking from the Barn Lawn past the Diana Stone and down the
transverse walk of the pyramidal cedars

Here, then is one of the three main "spines" of the garden. Along with the hedge-on-sticks walk and the *potager* walk, it gives the garden its definition and provides, even in the winter, an attractive structure. As supporting members of the gardens' growth, they seem always to be suggesting further elaboration and expansion. But I had begun in 1985 with the idea of perimeter walks round the farm, and this year saw the beginnings of one of them: the eastern walk. Some forty or so maples, planted in the usual rainy April weather by my friend Craig Patterson, formed about half of that walk. Some of them complemented the poplars that had been planted by the road and that were already flourishing.

Another of my "students" in the garden-history course I gave that winter was an alumna who owned a tree farm in Caledon. She had offered me as many white pines as I wanted for the mere cost of digging them up. So, one day in early April, Ron and I went in a rented truck and spent the day, first loading the poor victims into the truck and spraying them to keep their micro-roots alive, and then driving the sixty-mile-dash to Stonyground to get them all planted — more than a hundred in total — as quickly as possible.

And how splendid they looked! No need to wait for those seedling pines to grow; they could be replanted around Barn Lawn. Here was the garden suddenly "walled" with its hedge of feathers. Things are rarely so easy in the garden, and horticultural pride is often quickly followed by blight. "Study like Helen Phail", we used to write in our high-school textbooks. There's a lot of that in gardening too, on whatever scale. The inital euphoria at the full-grown hedges in the Great Garden began gradually to give way to despair as the summer wore on. Water as I might, one tree after another (though not all of them) capitulated to that summer's blazing heat. I felt I understood Pope's similar anguish over his garden at Twickenham in 1723: "My body is sick, my soul is troubled, my pockets are empty, my time is lost, my trees are withered, my grass is burned! So ends my history." But I was brought up on the story of Robert the Bruce and the spider, trying, failing, and trying again to make its web. And this, after all, was Bruce County.

Because white pines are very susceptible to a rust borne by currants and gooseberries, I subsequently removed all of these fruit bushes from the *potager* to the lower orchard — as far away as possible. But the damage (though not complete) was already done, and even now occasionally one of the trees will turn up its toes unexpectedly. Fortunately, the hedge is now big and bushy enough to entertain an occasional loss and accept a junior stand-in, but I am reconciled to its eventual replacement with spruce: not so lush but far more hardy.

For all its set-backs, I think that the summer of '88 was the first time that I felt that the garden was taking shape. One now arrived in a paved forecourt facing an elegant garden building (the pump-house), saw a hedged garden of

An old terracotta tile at the steps next to
the rose garden beyond the *potager*

Opposite The pumphouse and white garden

considerable size to the right and a lawn beginning to take shape under old apple trees next to it. And to the left was a broad walk that took you up to the house, past a long border that was beginning to look as it was supposed to do. The house and the barn were now connected by the gardens, gardens that I knew would suggest (as they grew) that they had always been here.

Sometimes visitors have suggested how lucky I was to inherit all these gardens. Of course, they are completely wrong, but I love the sense that the gardens now convey of being lucky survivals from a more gracious time. The Italian Renaissance had a nice word for this: *sprezzatura*. It's hard to translate into English, but it suggests the ability to do something of great difficulty or complexity as if it had cost no effort at all. That's what I'd like to have here. I hate even to be caught mowing the lawn.

But that most pedestrian of gardening jobs was becoming (along with weeding) more than I could handle. Already there was the tediousness of several big lawns to be mowed . . . and more in the making, and so I began to look about for the first of my gardeners. An inquiry to my neighbour led to his niece, an "Aggie" (agricultural student) who was reputed to be a hard worker. And so Michelle was, though she had had no experience with *this* part of agriculture. I may ostensibly have been the expert, but I think we found out many things together as we tried to plant and maintain both the flower and the vegetable gardens. One of the solutions — mulching — I was not to try until many years later.

That summer I also began to extend the gardens beyond the potager. The compost yard was already in place there and, across from it, the nursery, under the one apple tree that had not been sacrificed to the hedge-on-sticks walk. But there was nothing to connect this part of the garden to the Great Garden. A new cross walk (with steps) had to be built, and next to it (the following year) a limestone wall supporting an upper garden for old shrub roses. All of this was part of a project that only seven years later is coming to a conclusion with the building beyond the barn of a terrace and rockery, new steps and beds.

CHAPTER 6

Look Down to Water

Lakes, Beds, and Arbours

What is more pleasure, first thing in spring: the snowdrops and aconites, or the Easter rooster stuffed with wild leeks and roasted slowly all day in the woodstove? Made in 1910 in Brantford by the William Buck Co., the stove has been heating the house and cooking the dinners for three-quarters of a century. By now I had begun to understand that stove and the knowledge that comes with it: what I call "rival knowledge", a knowledge quite apart from the world of systems, switches, and dials. This is the sort of knowledge that allows you to know when the soil is ready for planting or a plant needs moving.

The woodstove has to be understood; it cannot be learned in a credit-course. Gradually you come to know what wood burns best and what hottest, what is best for baking and what for heating. You know by walking past, even without pausing, whether it is hot enough for the task you set it. My grandmother had talked about working pie pastry until it was "shotty": a word that mystified me for years until I realized it meant "like small shot" or what we know now as "BBs". It is a knowledge only at your finger's ends. This, too, is the gardener's knowledge.

It is a knowledge that came late to me, this willingness to listen, to wait. When it did, it became an inscription: the first text that you see when you arrive in the garden. Italian gardens of the Renaissance had a *lex hortum* ("rules of the garden") at the entrance: "Don't pick the flowers", "Stay on the walks", and so on. Stonyground has one. There it is in the curved brick wall that hides the cars from the house, the single Latin word *Attende*: "Wait", "Pay attention." I suppose it is T.S. Eliot's sense of the garden in *The Four Quartets* too: a place where secrets will be yielded up only to the inquiring and attentive eye. Here meanings will always lurk, waiting to be discovered, as Mary Lennox discovers the lost key and the little door to the garden of wonders in Frances Hodgson Burnett's famous classic children's book *The Secret Garden*.

Like Pavlov's dog, my mind offers these recollected associations continually. Some of them become inscriptions, some not. That summer I was writing an article on Andrew Marvell's poem "Upon Appleton House": the first record of an Englishman's recognition that the landscape is also a garden. Marvell has provided several texts for my landscape, but perhaps none is so apposite as the one that now sits at

Andrew Marvell quotation at the border
of garden and landscape

the edge of the west lawn, just as you walk into the meadow. "Abbyss", it says, in Marvell's spelling: a signal that you are about to pass across an abyss from the fixed architectural formalities of the garden into the true abbeys of nature.

The first text to be inscribed in the garden itself preceded *Attende* and "Abbyss" by several years. That was the Pope installation that had been suggested to me by my friend Peter Day in 1989. Peter, whose greatest memorial is the wonderful Calatrava arcade that he suggested for BCE Place in Toronto, was an art consultant and had taken an evening course in garden history that I gave to the alumnae/i of my college the previous winter. From that he recognized immediately what I was up to in all this: that my gardening was a sort of history of the history of gardens. And so nothing less would do than a series of installations to suggest that.

The first was to be a nod to Pope, one of the great apologists, practitioners, and theorists of the eighteenth-century garden. Peter knew that Pope's garden had been destroyed after his death by Lady Howe, whose husband also managed to lose America in the Revolutionary War! Peter imagined that we might have found the remains of the great obelisk that stood at the far end of that garden. This was Pope's monument to his mother: *Ah Editha, Matrum optima, mulierum amantissima, vale* ("O Edith, best of mothers, most beloved of women, farewell"). In fact, that obelisk had not been destroyed with the garden; it is now in a garden in Buckinghamshire. But the idea was a nice one and Peter set about to realize it.

First he collected some large marble fragments from a house renovation near his Toronto home. Then he brought them to the farm, where we laid them out on a piece of plywood so as to form the parts of a notional rectangle. Tobey then lettered the plywood rectangle with Pope's text and proceeded to work out which bits of which letters went on which fragment. After all that, the carving and the setting of this inscription into the main walk to the house seemed almost an anticlimax!

There was another inscription that year, a quotation from Coleridge's poem "This Lime-Tree Bower My Prison". It's a great favourite of mine, and a poem whose first lines always come into my mind just as departing visitors step down from the house into the main walk:

Well, they are gone, and here must I remain,
This lime-tree bower my prison! . . .

Just by those steps, on either side, there are two basswoods: regrowths from the stumps of two old trees that I had had to cut down just after I came in 1984. Basswoods are our native lindens, what the English call "limes", and just at midday they perform on the walk the dance of shadows that Coleridge describes:

. . . Pale beneath the blaze
Hung the transparent foliage; and I watch'd
Some broad and sunny leaf, and loved to see

The shadow of the leaf and stem above
Dappling its sunshine! . . .

So at that point is a flagstone inscribed in a cursive script with those first four words: my text now in what the Romans called a *locus amoenus*, a special place set apart.

There were to be other texts like that in the walks round the landscape too: texts that Peter showed me that spring and that he subsequently had made in enamel on steel. You come upon them, in what look like bird-boxes, but with names on them, as you go round. "Clare" says one in the hedgerow of the main avenue to the woods. And when you open it, there is the Romantic poet John Clare's wonderful comment on his work: "I found my poems in the fields and only wrote them down."

There the wild mixes with the tame, art with nature, as it does in Clare's early poem about his native village, Helpstone:

Thou far-fled pasture long evanish'd scene
Where nature's freedom spread the flowery green
Where golden kingcups open'd in to view
Where silver dazies charm'd the 'raptur'd' view
And tottering hid amidst those brighter gems
Where silver grasses bent their tiny stems
Where the pale lilac mean and lowly grew
Courting in vain each gazer's heedless view
While cowslaps sweetest flowers upon the plain
Seemingly bow'd to shun the hand in vain.

Clare, who knew botanical Latin, was as keen a champion of local dialect names for plants as was Robert Burns. I treasure him as the tutelary genius of regional words for things here also: the opposition to Disneyfication. Think of our own local names: "Devil's cup" for the little mushroom that sits like a drop of blood on the bare logs of March; mayflower and Dutchman's breeches; and even that garden escapee, sweet rocket, that now fills empty meadows and that the garden writer Louise Beebe Wilder tells me was once known as "Queen's Gillyflower". What Clare called "kingcups" we call "marsh marigold", but it is good to find it polyseminally inhabiting the language with fifty-six different names.

This is why a book like Geoffrey Grigson's *The Englishman's Flora* is such an engaging read. Recognizing that most of our garden flowers were once "wild", Grigson's wide survey includes not only the wild and the tame but the native and the introduced, and with each plant the wonderful litany of local names it has been given. Take that scourge of our rural gardens, shepherd's purse. Introduced by accident or sentimentality into North America, it has an ancient lineage. John Clare was a gardener, but he had a good word for this weed nonetheless:

E'en here my simple feelings nurse
A love for every simple weed
And e'en this little shepherds purse

Grieves me to cut it up — Indeed
I feel at times a love and joy
For every weed and every thing
A feeling kindred from a boy
A feeling brought with every spring.

Grigson is fond of citing Clare in his book, though his entry for shepherd's purse does not. What he does give is the huge litany of invented names that our English-speaking culture has created for this one plant: Bad Man's Oatmeal, Blindweed, Caseweed, Casewort, Crow-Pecks, Fat Hen, Gentleman's Purse, Guns, Hens and Chickens, Lady's Purses, Money-Bags, Mother's Heart, Naughty Man's Plaything, Old Woman's Bonnet, Pepper and Salt, Pick-Your-Mother's-Heart-Out, Pickpocket to London, Poor Man's Pharmacetty, Poor Man's Purse, Poverty Purse, Purseflower, Rifle the Ladies' Purses, Shepherd's Pedlar, Shepherd's Pocket, Shepherd's Pouch, Shepherd's Scrip, Snake-Flower, Stony-in-the-Wall, Tacker Weed.

Someone once wrote that you can tell where you are in Great Britain by the local verb used for making tea: "mash", "brew", "draw", "infuse", "steep", and so on. "Language best shows a man. Speak that I may know you," said Shakespeare's contemporary Ben Jonson. Anyone who has been lucky enough as a child to be taken through the spring woods and told the names of all the flowers there will know how variable these can be. Our names, even for our towns, tell us who we are. The words we use for ordinary

The "Rule of the Garden" in the wall by the carpark

Opposite The Coleridge inscription in the long walk near the house

things, not least for weeds, tell us where we came from. They also tell us something about our own inventiveness.

What deep longing for home led the settlers to call our thrush a robin, when it has nothing to do with the little English robin? And what led them to call *Arisaema triphyllum* "Jack-in-the-pulpit" when it looks so similar to that English spring flower Lords and Ladies (in fact a different species, *Arum maculatum*)? The other common name for Lords and Ladies is "Cuckoo-pint", another flower that Clare was fond of. And "Cuckoo-pint" is one of the names that was used in Canada for Jack-in-the-pulpit, though it did not stick as the common name. Neither did the great long list of other names that Charlotte Erichsen-Brown gives for Jack-in-the-pulpit in her excellent book *Use of Plants* (a kind of *Canadians' Flora* without the gender bias). There we can find that it is (or was) also known as Indian Turnip, Wild Turnip, Marsh Pepper, Bog Onion, Brown Dragon, Starchwort, Dragon Root, and even Wake Robin, a name that is more commonly used now for the red trillium.

To look at the earliest Canadian flora, Jacques Cornut's *Canadensium Plantarum* (1636), is to get a sense of the vast horticultural confusion that this country's plants must have presented to the first European taxonomers. Poor Cornut, the keeper of the royal plant garden in Paris, had only the dried specimens sent back to him by the Jesuits. Small wonder that he thought our trillium was a nightshade, or that at least half a dozen of his identifications are unrecognizable to modern botanists!

One of the flowers that was here was our wayside lilac. It is so often found on the site of old farm buildings nowadays, we think of it as a sign of settlement and cultivation, made most memorable by Whitman in his elegy for President Lincoln:

When lilacs last in the dooryyard bloom'd,
And the great star early droop'd in the western sky in the night,
I mourn'd, and yet shall mourn with ever-returning spring.

Both a wild flower, then, and cultivated, lilac might as easily be in a garden as in a hedgerow. Clare understood that the hedgerows were the gardens of the fields. My Clare birdbox, with its hidden text, is in a hedgerow of hawthorns, a tree awash with white blossom in June, and in winter its silvery branches even more elegantly downed with white. (How infinitely preferable — and less destructive — a branch of it is as a Christmas tree than the clichéd conventionality of a conifer!) Just across from that quotation one of the lilacs dug out of the west lawn now flourishes nicely. I did not plan it to reflect on Clare, but I like to think he would have approved.

How often these ideas lie fallow, or come to fruition only years later! And how often I have been grateful for that, for my inability to rush ahead with a "spontaneous overflow of powerful feeling", as Wordsworth puts it. "Emotion recollected in tranquillity" is a better text for the gardener. Did I know that the set of harrows that I bought at the farm auction across the road that year would eventually turn into gates, for example? It was that same spring, by chance, that I also happened to be in Chesley, where Tobey lives, and to see in the cemetery there the wonderful rows of pyramidal cedars: our version of cypresses. Like something out of an Italian landscape, I thought, and so I tucked them away and began to think of where I might put such an avenue.

But gardening on this scale is not all reverie about inscriptions and avenues. There was a lot of good hard slog to be done that spring. First, the repairs. The mature pines hedging the Great Garden had not wintered well, and thirty of them needed to be replaced. Then there was the new rose border: an Allen Paterson suggestion to add to the gardens near the house. It was to go parallel to the long border and both to provide another way of walking through that area and to take the eye gradually outward from the house towards a more open landscape.

To begin with, the long border was to be backed with a lattice fence — for height and winter definition — on which climbers would be planted. This, then, would be a transition to a forty-foot bed containing a range of shrub roses underplanted with tulips. Sporting magnificent rosehips in the autumn and winter, these statuesque old roses that even hold the snow in interesting ways are a million miles from Allen Paterson's description of hybrid tea roses for most of the year in our climate: "three sticks and a hill of dirt".

This rose bed would involve redoing the lawn in that area, long overdue after the removal of what was left of the old original border. It would also entail removing the stump of an old maple that had blown down the previous autumn, and the rail fence that I had put up to prevent contractors from driving across the lawn to the house, as they seemed to expect to do.

Fortunately, this job could be integrated with two others. The sod from the rose bed could go to creating a terrace on the south side of the house from which eventually a stair will lead down into the new orchard there. And at least some of the soil, plus the spring clean-up from the gardens generally and a healthy load of my cousin's barnyard special, could go to the making of a new vegetable garden west of the *potager*: a garden for all those vegetables that don't look particularly pretty in a formal arrangement — potatoes and squash and corn. Terraced into the hill, the garden is called "Gugliano", after the terraces at the Tuscan farmhouse of my friend Myra, and I've just added a rail fence and grapevine to complete the picture.

Nineteen-eighty-nine was also the year of the arbour, the structure now planted with grape that connects the pump-house to the Great Garden and provides a directed focus on the main walk from the house to the barn. Made of cedar uprights and rails, it was another demonstration of the value of small rural industry. We had used squared timbers for the pergola on the back of the house, but that was architectural, and this, it seemed, should be more rustic, more substantial. No large lumber outfit could supply logs twelve feet long, and yet the local sawmill could and did. And it has been local industry that has continued to provide so much of what is needed in a garden on this scale. My gardener Michelle's father brought his tractor-driven post-hole–digger, and the arbour and the lattice fence went in.

Well, perhaps the operation was not so easy as all that. My notes speak of aching belly muscles from the digging and lifting. But the increasing order of the whole is an encouragement, the sense that the bones sustain, and bit by bit the weeds are kept at bay. Always, though, there is the desperation of that month and a half in April and early May: maples to transplant into the rest of the eastern avenue, new conifers to plant in the shelterbelts, seedlings to be nurtured towards transplanting into the *potager*, limestone ledgerock to be ordered for more borders, trees to be replaced or added to in the orchard.

Early spring is a time of madness; even the jackrabbits run crazy races through the alfalfa. Maybe it's that intensity, and perhaps the waiting for full spring to break, that causes one to see more clearly and rejoice in the little bulbs that the chipmunks have spared: *Pulchella violacea,* the white-winged snowdrops, chionodoxa, and the scillas in blue and white.

And then suddenly, it seems, it's the Herb Fair at Durham: basil and dill and summer savory, and some new oddity like pineapple sage. Out goes the lady's-mantle under the lindens in the hedge-on-sticks. In goes a new cedar hedge around the west lawn, to replace the "tapestry" hedge of

One of John Clare's sayings on a tree in the old fencerow
of the main walk to the woods

blue beech that hadn't taken. Planted in well-dug cow manure, it breaks the wind in that new hilltop space and offers vistas: the distant view of my cousin's barn and silos looking, in the wonderful misty goldenlight of autumn, like an Italian Renaissance church with two towers.

Some things, some of the best things, come by chance: my neighbour Bob offering me some great slabs of local limestone from the ancient riverbed of the Saugeen, for example. Removed by a contractor who was making a sub-division in the town, they were too good to use just for fill, and they have become the steps and entrances for the parts of the garden on the edges: the transitions to the landscape where something too regular would be inappropriate.

It was as I was talking to Bob about all this that another neighbour stopped to make conversation. If your family has lived in one place for 120 years, it is likely that you'll be related to a lot of people. Frannie Riley was one of those "sort-of-cousins" whose relationship no one can quite figure out. Several years earlier he and his brother had cleared one of my fields of stone with their self-invented stone-picking machine. The stone went into my barnyard to turn it from a bog into a car park, but not before I had asked Frannie about making a "lake" at the bottom of the hill below the house, in a bit of swamp that was mosquito heaven.

"Well, what about that pond?" he said when he saw me, and two days later he arrived at the crack of dawn with the bulldozer in tow. Scrambling my wits together I stood behind him, directing as he drove through brush and trees, and within the day the first stage of the "lake" had been made. "It should be called 'Lake Islay'," said Campbell, remembering the single-malt that we had tried on a visit to the ancestral ground in Scotland the previous year, and so it was.

The whole operation took more than a bulldozer and more than a day. The excavator was not finished with the operation until the autumn, but when the water came, it came strongly. "Well, she won't be a dry hole, anyway," said Frannie, whose own well had been driven dry by the expansion of the town's deep well next door. That was the summer of the film *Manon des Sources,* and the welling-up of the spring water into the excavation had the same primitive magic that is quite inexpressible. Only when the stony spoil from the bed had been shaped around the pond into an Ojibway water-dragon did I feel the spirit of all that had been appeased.

And there was still one more appeasement, one naming, to be done. One of my great-aunt's stories was of the day of the emigration, the day when her father, his brother, and their father had gone for the last time to inspect the sheep that had been in their care. Rowing back from the island of Scarba, they got caught in the current between it and Jura, a current that led straight to the second-largest whirlpool in the world, Corrievrechan. It was a current that very nearly did in George Orwell about a hundred years later when he was living there, writing *1984.* "It's all over boys," said my great-grandfather, throwing down his oars. "Row! Row!" said my great-great-uncle Angus, and so they got out and came to Canada. What he said, of course, as he spoke only Gaelic, was "Imrich, imrich," and I shall not be happy until I have an old wooden rowboat called *Imrich* on that pond.

The past is not a burden at Stonyground, but it is part of its text: my text, the text of my mother's generation, and a much longer generation going back as far as naming and memory. In a computer world such as ours, where everything is zero or one, yesterday or today, the process of a garden is a difficult concept, and the process of how a landscape comes to mean, almost an impossibility. My father's earliest memory was of the bells in his village church in eastern Ontario ringing for the relief of the siege of Ladysmith in the Boer War. His aunt was older than the country. To most of my students these relatives might as well have been living in the Roman Republic. In a sense, of course, they were; Roman culture was still their culture, and the boys at the village school could call a local Gypsy "Old Queen Dido" without needing a footnote to tell them who that was. This is the perspective in which one makes a garden such as this, one that I shall never see in its fullness: a place of venerable trees and ancient peace.

During that summer, the railway that had crossed the farm for more than one hundred years was removed. Latterly it had been used only to carry mysterious cargo back and forth to the Bruce Nuclear Generator, so my attitude to its passing was slightly mixed. But it was, after all, part of the place, and stories about it and its construction were part of the farm's history; its track was part of the farm's landscape.

Four times a day the trains had come and gone — two passenger, two freight — sometimes letting off my great-aunts from Chicago at the crossing below the hill. The building of the railway had been the first instance of a cash economy in a world run by barter, and its construction was legendary, with epic battles. From it, men had paid off the mortgages on their farms or brawled their way into drunken ruin. With it, the market economy of agriculture in the county had been constructed. In its ancient stuffed coaches, we had travelled to the farm in the winter and, on its freight, my grandmother had sent down a goose and two ducks every Christmas. As a child, in those pre-electric days, I had imagined the howling night train leaving its tracks and coming to get me in the dark farm bedroom in which we were not allowed to have an oil lamp for fear of fire. Now, with a monstrous machine that backed down the tracks swallowing the rails, it was gone, leaving the right-of-way rapidly falling to dirt-bikers and other noise machines.

CHAPTER 7

Et in Arcadia Ego

Avenues and Memorials

In the midst of Poussin's painting *The Shepherds of Arcadia*, the inhabitants of an idyllic landscape look at a monument on which is carved the text (in Latin): "I too have been in Arcadia." The "I" is death, the mother of beauty, as the poet Wallace Stevens called her, "since from her all things spring". It is not easy to read that lesson: that without the losses of time and death we would not cherish the moments of beauty. In 1990 three of my friends died from AIDS-related illnesses, and a fourth was Peter Day, who had been so much an inspiration and begetter of the projects for Stonyground. I found myself coming back to the farm after the funeral of one and bursting into tears at the beauty of the place. Who, then, was this garden to be for among "these waves of dying friends"?

Part of gardening is a defiance of death, of transitoriness, of destruction. "Once more, ye muses, and once more," Milton wrote in the first line of "Lycidas", the greatest elegy in the language, defying time to stop his voice. And so the seasons begin again, and one goes on. I think of my two great-aunts reciting poetry: one of them shouting Shelley's "Ode to the West Wind" at the violence of April, the other declaiming Ulysses's rejection of despair in Tennyson's poem:

Push off, and sitting well in order smite
The sounding furrows; for my purpose holds
To sail beyond the sunset, and the baths
Of all the western stars, until I die.

And so the seasons begin again, as Tennyson also recognized in "In Memoriam"; one goes on. The projects for the year were already in place. Michelle was to return, but not until May, so April was a month of fury. Thank God for willing students! One of them, Michael Holmes, now a successful poet, came up and helped me move spruces from the overpopulated shelterbelt to fill gaps in the Great Garden hedge. As the temperature in April shot up to 30°C, we worked madly in the Great Garden to replace the Japanese crab-apples and the espaliered apricots that rabbits had girdled. And with equal demonic speed we replaced the maples in the avenues that had not made it through the winter.

O nature! Only the urban-dweller with racoons in the attic knows the ambiguity of response it can provoke in the countryman. I had spared a nest of little rabbits the year before, feeding them and transporting them several miles away to a swamp. This year I was ready to murder every Raggylug among them, and the groundhogs and chipmunks too. What a good thing for them — and the marauding dirt-bikers too — that I had not yet bought a rifle! This, though, was the year I began to think that a fence for the *potager* would be a good idea.

Sometimes the race seems not so much to the swift as to the thug, whether human or otherwise: the groundhogs already putting landmines in the serpentine path that I was making to the pond, the labourer-hooligans tearing up the railway and wantonly destroying a kildeer's nest on the disused railbed, my neighbour's new driving range peppering my tranquil walks with golfballs. Unannounced invaders even come in with a load of innocuous-looking topsoil: the green tansy mustard in the orange quadrant of the Great Garden or the creeping Charlie appearing to take over the east lawn. But then there are the compensations too: the Hydro employees who arrive unannounced with a gift-load of shredded tree branches for mulch, or my cousin wth a load of vermiculated limestone for a corner of the Great Garden.

The mulch was a legacy of the first group to visit the garden: the local horticultural society who had come the year before to see the work-in-progress and be bewildered by it. Among them, as I maundered on about the dearth of decent mulch, was a Hydro supervisor always on the lookout for somewhere to dump wood chips at the end of the day . . . and, it turned out, only too happy to oblige. Such, such are the perks of garden life in the country.

As ever, it is the projects that keep one going on: "Gugliano" to finish edging with the wooden ties bought from the railway demolition gang; a new bed of irises and other things to plan for next to the car park; first speculations on an upper swimming pond in the old gravel pit on the hill. The last was where Peter Day's assistant, Brad Golden, came into the picture: a bright and engaged young landscape architect who had got his mind past foundation plantings and knew how to line such a pond to make it watertight.

Sometimes it's just as well that one has neither the energy nor the money to do everything at once. That dodo of Canadian government, the Senate, may have been meant to encourage "sober second thoughts", but that does not mean that all second thoughts are a bad thing. In fact, the upper pond has never been made. Year after year, a season's worth of brush and woody perennials needs to be burned there, and somehow that site slides to the bottom of a list that is always full of more urgent screaming. And when do I ever get to swim — the original intention for this upper pond?

As I write this, it seems more likely now that it will become a water garden, to complement another new garden on that hill . . . and that there will be a pergola at the top for grapes. On this southwest-facing, gravelly slope, there, if anywhere, grapes will prosper. Images of slippered contemplation among the ripening vines, a place to sit in the evening . . . these are almost enough to stifle the realities of groundhogs and mosquitoes.

It was Brad, too, who knew that Peter had left me a marble watering-can. Heavy enough to require two men to carry it, it nonetheless looked convincing at a distance, so the joke was to position it by the new path to the pond, just far enough beyond the west lawn to look as if it might have been left out there by mistake. But I also spotted Peter's Beatrix Potter joke in giving it to me; I was Mr. McGregor, he the rabbit hiding in the symbolic watering-can. It was time for Tobey again, and a few weeks later the can reappeared with "*Petrus*" carved on the side: a sort of maker's mark to the casual eye, but to the Latinist a signal that this can was stone. Without knowing it, though, Tobey compounded the joke by adding a tail to the "r", thereby creating the word "*rus*" (countryside) as if the can were also a signpost to the landscape.

And so it is, for it sits beyond the lawn just as one steps over "Abbyss" from the "smooth-shaven green" of the lawn into the serpentine path through the long grass of the field. Perhaps one day I shall try to turn that field into one of those Christopher Lloyd–style meadows, full of wild flowers and just the grasses one wants.

That kind of naturalizing, though, is never as easy as the nurseries like to pretend. What it takes to be effective is a thorough ploughing down (and probably spraying to eliminate couch grass) before the "canvas" of the fields is ready to receive the genteel wild flowers that our culture has decided are not weeds. And if you intend to underplant with bulbs, as I have here and there, you need to reckon on leaving the long grass unmown for at least two months in the spring: an untidiness that will alarm your neighbours and probably bring down upon you the wrath of the weed-hunting township authorities.

What a lot the seed companies have to answer for with their "meadows in a can" or the bulb suppliers with their "ideal for naturalizing" . . . and the banks, too, with their naïve images of rural retirement to five careless acres and a dog! How much more likely, in our landscape, to end up with a field full of burdock and thistle, with the occasional sad poppy to mark the failed attempt! Year by year, the daffodils put on their early display on my hill only to be overwhelmed by a sheet of "me too" dandelions gearing up for their annual invasion of the garden. Where I have seriously tried to eliminate them, I have had to cultivate the field and plant it with rye grass, which makes a heavy-enough blanket to keep down that weed, which the French (much more accurately) call "piss in the bed".

Petrus was a signal to me, however, to begin doing something about that proposed hill-meadow — at least ridding it of its weedy thorns and fallen branches, enhancing its curving charms with a broad serpentine walk but sparing its one wonderful clump of wild asparagus. "Brian's Walk" it is now called, after Brian Norbury, the man with whom I

Marble watering can in memory of Peter Day
Opposite The Harrow Gates by the carpark

have shared nearly half my life, who suggested it and who himself worked away that summer to create it. Nowadays it winds greenly downhill, through the meadow grasses and past old apple trees and a hedgerow of walnuts and old spruces, towards the disused railway and the pond, pausing at the bottom with another quotation suggested by Peter.

That one was more complex. Suggested by the metal "s" that used to be found in railway ties to hold them together, my idea drew upon two of the great aestheticians of the early eighteenth century: William Hogarth and William Kent. Kent, the friend of Pope and creator of Rousham, had said that "nature abhors a straight line". Hogarth had elaborated the notion on the title-page of his *Analysis of Beauty,* where a (female) serpentine line was contained inside a (male) geometrical shape. Here, then, was a serpentine walk meeting a straight line, the railway. What better place for a sort of "landscape engraving" celebrating the origins of the idea? And so, inside a gravelled rectangle outlined with ledgerock, the end of a railway tie, with its metal "s", was sunk vertically. Inside the ledgerock frame it became the "subject" to be "signed" in the appropriate corners with the autographs (in stone) of Kent "the painter" and Hogarth "the engraver" of the piece.

This project, of course, led to the need for a path beyond the railway to make the connection with the lake. This path, in turn, became part of a longer walk there that wanders off through the woods to link up with the other walk down from the house. Meandering as it does beside the lake but never arriving on its banks, it seemed the right place for another inscription, one suitable to a handsome flat piece of pink granite that had turned up on the site of the proposed upper pond when the berm was made there.

The path is a wandering delusion, a mistake; you ought to have turned right in order to get to the pond. And yet it is a pretty mistake, for there are some rhododendrons under the pines. In Latin the word *error* means "to wander" and Milton plays with its pleasing ambiguity in *Paradise Lost* when he gives us one of the most beautiful similes in the poem, only to cancel it. It is the description, appropriately, of the fall of Mulciber, the architect of heaven itself:

Men call'd him Mulciber; and how he fell
From Heav'n, they fabl'd, thrown by angry Jove
Sheer o're the Crystal Battlements: from Morn
To Noon he fell, from Noon to dewy Eve,
A Summer's day; and with the setting Sun
Dropt from the Zenith like a falling Star,
On Lemnos th'Ægean Isle: thus they relate,
Erring . . .

So, as one of Milton's contemporaries says in a poem of the same period, a "sweet mistake . . . mistake, tho false, intending true".

These were not to be the only new paths. My encounter with pyramidal cedars the previous year had lain fallow, waiting for an occasion, and now it presented itself.

Looking east out of the Great Garden, I recognized that what was needed to extend its bounds and "call in the country" (as Pope had recommended) was an avenue stretching beyond the Diana stone six hundred feet to the eastern boundary, where a clump of wild cherry and apple in the old hedgerow conveniently closed the view. Within a week or two I had gathered up the last remaining stock of cedars from a nurserywoman in Chesley and planted most of the avenue: the trees (those potential columns) thirty feet apart so that the farm machinery could go back and forth across the avenue between them.

I suppose it must have been about that time that I began to imagine a temple at the end of that vista: the sort of circular structure that's usually called a "temple of the winds" but which in this case would be a temple to Ceres, the goddess of the harvest that would surround it. It would be a dwarf silo, between fifteen and twenty feet tall, surrounded with a peristyle of columns: all of it made of poured concrete and sand-blasted to look like stone. And no, it would not be any old Ceres either, but the mourning Ceres, Ceres looking for her lost daughter Proserpina in the Underworld, as Eve is first described in *Paradise Lost*. On the interior walls would be carved the names of my friends who had died, mostly in the Great War with AIDS. Somewhere, perhaps, there would be Wilfred Owen's line about that earlier war — "and half the seed of Europe, one by one" — and in the centre of the floor, perhaps, beneath the opening in the dome, the lines from Gray's "Elegy" that had jumped out at me when I had read them at Peter's funeral: "And melancholy marked him for her own."

Well, that has yet to come about. There are limits to the madness that one's bank manager allows in any one year! What was done that year (and at almost no expense) was the creation of the memorial to my mother. Named for my great-aunt Margaret who had lived here almost until her death at the age of ninety-nine, my mother had always loved this place, but she had died before her aunt, and so never lived to see it become her own home. Now she was to be here, in the grove of elms on the eastern walk, to which Campbell tugged from his farm (her birthplace) with his 150-horsepower tractor an enormous piece of erratic granite.

There, among the elms, we cut a circular glade and put the stone in it, carved with a spray of marguerites to name her. All this was, of course, another poem: Gerard Manley Hopkins's "Spring and Fall". As the elm leaves turn golden in the autumn, the poem comes into its own: "Margaret, are you grieving / Over Goldengrove unleaving?"

Not everything that year was elegiac though. In the high summer I cleaned out the old path in the woods and extended it. And this was the first year that I began seriously to follow Southcote's advice to rifle the garden for the hedgerows and to plant in the avenues the flowers that I had thinned from the gardens. Alex Wilson, a landscape designer and the author of *The Culture of Nature*, came up and approved. I felt I was getting somewhere.

The serpentine walk to the lake

Opposite The monument to my mother in the grove

All that summer I was finishing the book that I had started when I was on sabbatical in the spring of 1989. Called *The Planters of the English Landscape Garden*, it was my attempt to put the gardeners back into gardening, to illustrate that the great gardens of England were not made simply by owners and designers but by nurserymen, gardeners, and botanists. Here, more than anything, my two lives had come together: writing about gardening and doing it. Here were the gardens and the gardeners that had inspired me, long before I owned Stonyground, and here was I now, writing about them in the morning and gardening in the afternoon.

It seemed — it was — a great happiness, and a necessary escape from the mortality that overshadowed that year. But that happiness is impossible to explain to a culture that puts work on one side and play on the other, thereby reducing life to a wash-cycle of drudgery and exhilaration. I remember one Christmas as I was going off to England for the break, one of my neighbours had asked me how I was spending it. "You academics are so lucky," he said. "All those holidays." When I explained that I would be spending three of the four weeks in the British Library, working on my research, he was astonished. "So you're not having a holiday, then?" he said.

A few days later I was coming out of the Manuscripts Room of the British Library on a dark rainy December evening. The library was closing, and I was to meet my friend Craig, who had been working in printed books, and we were to go across the road to the Museum Tavern. Over a good pint I would tell him what I had found that day (some amazing seventeenth-century letters about gardens) and he would tell me about his research into early eighteenth-century criminals. And I was enormously happy in a way that would take eternity to explain to my neighbour.

But then, what do most of my casual visitors say? "So much work!" As if work of this kind were a grind, like what is now most of the workplace. "I had rather be shovelling real bull shit," I once said to Campbell, "than dealing with the metaphorical kind that goes on nowadays in the classroom. At least the flowers like the real stuff, and blossom."

CHAPTER 8

Concealing the Bounds

Walls and Gates

"Rest rusts" had already become the text for Stonyground, long before it was installed next to the Rousham seat in the orange quadrant of the Great Garden in 1991. Suggested to me by a Dutch garden-historian friend, its text is cut out in Dutch in rusty steel like a large plant label: a Dutch proverb, and so a suitable invocation of a nation of gardeners. It stands like a silent admonition: "Rest for a while, yes, but there's weeding to be done."

First thing that spring I had got some local contractors with a "cherrypicker" crane to take down the rest of a Manitoba maple behind the house. Its unstable branches had long been a concern, but, more to the point, its limbs were curtailing the growth of the handsome purple beech that my great-uncle had planted there early in the century. Because it branched near the base, half of the maple had been easy to cut down the previous year, but the other half leaned too close to the house to be sure that a chain-saw would make it fall the right way. Down it came with the crane, its rings revealing that it was even older than the house and must have been spared for the sake of its shade when the house was built in the 1870s.

Once it was down, however, I began to think about this unsatisfactory north side of the house. Windowless and mean, the house on this side turned its behind into the prevailing northwest wind, just as the cows do. Nothing of the garden was visible from the house, except from the bathroom upstairs. And the little terrace that I had made beyond the old woodshed on that side served only to draw attention to what now seemed a very unsatisfactory bit of the garden indeed. I began to think, and those thoughts proved to be expensive.

In the meantime, though, there was more than building work to think about. Another season of gardening had begun and there were more mundane things to be getting on with. Another maple, on the west side of the garden by the lane, had been taken down in a high wind the previous autumn, so there was much cutting up and burning to do. Windstorms, and even tornadoes, are a high risk in this part of the province. Two old maples that stand by the barn conceal in their leafy uppers the shattered limbs that took the brunt of a tornado in 1969 that would otherwise have destroyed the barn. No one in Bruce County is ever at ease with a wind from the south. It was just such a wind in

1870 that had carried burning brush from a farm being cleared across the road to land in a straw pile by the original barn. The men who had been building the house found that they had a new barn to build as well.

Not that the drama of the wind is not one of the great spectaculars at Stonyground. Frequently the clouds at one level are fleeing in the opposite direction from ones five hundred feet higher: the effect of the argument between competing weather systems. And often, especially in the autumn, as the leaves are turning, the clouds send sheets of flying luminescence over the distant woodlands, like a kind of landscape diorama. "A Fair luminous cloud" is a phrase of Coleridge's, that great poet of light and its effects, as if he were describing the cloud studies of his great contemporary Constable. Just such clouds are one of autumn's pleasures, but so too are the distant thunderheads of summer, piled high like the cloud castles of Maxfield Parrish's illustrations for the children's poems of Eugene Field. In winter too, it is the howling of the relentless northwest wind through the old spruces and against the house that makes the cheeriness of the Buck's Happy Thought woodstove the more intense, the intimate intensity that the American poet Elizabeth Bishop caught in her brilliant poem "Sestina":

> *September rain falls on the house.*
> *In the failing light, the old grandmother*
> *sits in the kitchen with the child*
> *beside the Little Marvel Stove,*

reading the jokes from the almanac,
laughing and talking to hide her tears.

It is Masefield's "mad March winds", though, that we face at tree-planting time, with their horizontal sleeting keenness. (And, as usual, there were seedling conifers to plant into the shelterbelt and the hedge of Barn Lawn that spring. And there was manuring, and digging, and plants to be moved about from bed to bed in an attempt to get the colour schemes right.) It was the first time that I began to wonder how long I would be able to carry on at this pace. Another early spring brought the apple blossom into a lusher fullness than I had ever seen it, but it also brought a record crop of mosquitoes and those little flies, known to the farmers as "no-see-ums", that seem to take a particular delight in getting into your eyes during planting season. Just as suddenly, everything was in bloom, tulips and peonies together; and the Black Parrot tulips in the oval garden were gone before you could notice.

As so often at Stonyground, the news of the great world seemed very far away indeed. The Gulf War went on, but the seventh year of the war with the groundhogs seemed more pressing, and the plans for a wall and some gates more meaningful. I had bricks left from an earlier project, a chimney replacement for which I had bought the remains of a demolished woodshed in the same brick as the house. And now that I had found a bricklayer who could build me a curved brick wall, it was the time to get on with the job of hiding the car park and giving the garden near the house some much-needed intimacy.

It seemed to take ages to persuade the one local man with a small backhoe to come to dig the foundation trench, but, once it was in, the wall as well as the gate piers for a new set of gates to the garden began to rise. The gates themselves were to be made from some old harrows that I had bought at auction, and that part of the job was to be the first project done for me by Tim Maycock, the man who has come to be far more than a gardener at Stony-ground. Trained as a glass-blower and metalworker, he is also an accomplished cabinet-maker and a gardener: a man in love with perfection and a joy to watch at work. He is not the only lucky "find" I have experienced in the course of making Stonyground, but he has had the most influence.

Michelle had gone off to marriage and motherhood, and although I had a high-school student working for me that summer, it was Tim I turned to when the hedge-on-sticks was finally ready for its first professional "haircut" with the hedge-trimmer. And it is he who has done that arm and back-aching job ever since. I have a less than ambiguous relationship with machinery, most of which instantly dies (or refuses to live) whenever I look at it. Tim, on the other hand, has a way of coaxing the wariest old lag of a machine into life. Indeed, he has a love of machinery that I could never acquire, humiliated as I have been by it since the earliest days' terror in front of a lathe in "manual training" at public school.

Tim was part of the "other culture" of the county that I stumbled upon almost by accident. The previous Christmas I had noticed some little reindeer made of twigs in the window of the Elora Soap Company in Paisley, a town that had begun to become interesting in the period since I came to Stonyground. In spite of being the birthplace of David Milne, Paisley had had a reputation for dour insularity: a history chronicled by the local Robin Hood, the bank-robber Micky Macarthur, in his autobiography, *I'd Rather Be Wanted than Had*. But now it had a fine bakery and deli, a good canoe store, and a liquor store with the largest collection of single-malts north of Toronto. And the Elora Soap Company sold much more than soap: lots of interesting local crafts — among them, it turned out, Tim's little deer.

I went in search of him in the even more improbable village of Cargill, and there I found him in an old Methodist church that he was resurrecting into a studio–workshop and house from its fifty-year slumber as a grain-store. I bore away a full-sized deer (for the woods by the pond) and a vase that looked as if a pheasant had come to rest in the glass. Now, several months later, he began to work Stonyground.

Framing for the harrow-gates was trickier, and more expensive, than it first seemed, but when the gates went in (glass handle and all), they fitted to a T and swung beautifully. It is hard to convey the sense of ceremoniousness such gates bestow on a garden: a sense that this place is an occasion.

Looking down the long border and rose border towards the house

Opposite Carpark border in spring with the gates beyond
and apple trees in bloom on Barn Lawn

"O enter then his gates with praise," they seem to say, like an announcement of celebration.

In fact, with their spiked bottoms pointing out aggressively towards the car park, these gates say, in effect, "Don't come this way. Go round by the arbour and the fountain." And that is what they are meant to say, for the lane behind them (made more attractive that spring by edging and levelling) is largely for us, the gardeners, to go back and forth to the barn.

What the gates also say, though, is: Here is the dignity of agriculture, and its beauty. Hung up so, at right angles, they have even fooled farmers who thought they recognized what a harrow was. But they are beautiful in their stark simplicity, and never more so than when the first wet snow sticks to their ribs and the whole shape of them comes suddenly alive.

All of this touches on the ceremonial, something that embarrasses Canadians and makes us nervous. And yet the countryside also has its ceremonies, its feasts and its exhibitions and fall fairs. And no one who remembers a threshing dinner can deny the ceremony of its parade of dishes, its pickles and relishes beautifully displayed, as lavish as a Lord Mayor's Feast. And sometimes at night, in the summer, after a long dinner and much wine, we go out with the citronella torchères and stroll the perimeter walk, like pilgrims to the dark mysteries that only an old cultivated landscape can have at night.

It was on one of these walks that Mildred first appeared, conjured out of the ether after a great feast and with a little assistance from what improving social workers like to call "substance". Mildred is the spirit of Brant Township: a caustic observer of manners and mores, and not least of the arty goings-on at Stonyground. Mildred's visitations never leave the guests (especially those from the city) unscathed. Impatient of affectation and what she calls "fol-de-rol", she seems to appear out of nowhere, though Campbell (whose ear is closer to the ground) always claims he can hear her approach.

That was the way she first appeared one autumn evening, just in time to deliver her famous Women's Institute lecture on the history of modern art as illustrated by a number of objects in the woods. There in the woods, lit only by flickering torches, she was able to conjure up the whole of modernism without a single reference to slides or videos or all the claptrap of the classroom. Guests who could scarcely remember anything about that evening the next day nonetheless talked for weeks afterwards about her particularly forceful account of *pointillisme* as illustrated by a particular stone in the woods.

If not exactly the "genius of the place", Mildred is certainly its spirit: the watchful guardian of common sense against the dangers of horticultural excess, and aestheticism generally. Self-advertised as a doer of good and visitor of the afflicted, Mildred is extensively acquainted with the greater world of (at least rural) Ontario, and her sharp tongue is no sparer of what she calls "nonsense and stuff". Her practical common sense has continued to haunt dinner parties late into the evening, though other dissident voices from the realm of the not-quite-supernatural have also begun to register their alternative visions of the place in one way or another, usually after a long meal at the end of a hard day's work.

That, of course, is for when friends come, and labour and enjoyment become part of a cycle that most people never see. My friend Myra, on a visit one summer, created what was to become "Chicken Stonyground": poached chicken breasts grilled with peppers and wild leeks and chopped wild ginger from the woods — tastes that she had remembered from another visit and made into a text of her own.

What a great discovery that ginger was! Unknown to my aunt Nellie, the accomplished home baker, it flourishes in her woods in thick carpets of heart-shaped leaves. Long after the wild leeks have sunk invisibly back to their underground bulbs in the summer, it is there for the picking. The roots, candied in sugar, or chopped into a vinaigrette on blanched snow peas or into a stir-fry of savoy cabbage and bavettes, have become a staple of the kitchen.

Dinner is the great time of day at Stonyground. I think of my friend Dennis, the professional baker whose exquisite desserts come to crown the meal that follows a day of step-building or stone-moving. "Flavoured with hunger sauce," my mother would have said; but such meals are also their ingredients: fresh peas and broad beans from the garden, with new potatoes and a salad of five different lettuces and all the range of herbs. And with them, a roast from the local butcher, the incomparable Batte's, with their four kinds of home-smoked sausages, smoked hams and bacon, and sweetbreads for the asking; or a butterfly leg of lamb from another local farmer, grilled with freshly picked mint, lemon, garlic, and olive oil on the wood barbecue. And afterwards, on July evenings, a summer pudding of fresh currants and gooseberries and raspberries served with *crème fraîche*. These are the things you can eat without fear of diet after a day of work.

But there is culinary competition. The bakery/deli in Paisley is run by another Elora refugee, Floreal, and that summer he put on two feasts of Basque food in one of the mills in the town. "Now I see why you spend all your time here in the summer," said a couple from Toronto I invited to one of those occasions. Flo's "Gateâux basques" have become a staple of the countryside now, though as often as not they're asked for as "ghetto-blasters".

The delights of this place are in all these things: scent, sight, taste, touch, even the sound of the bees. And it is most of all the sharing. One of the great pleasures has been to meet other gardeners, madmen (and -women) who have been smitten with its virus. Georg and Karen Maier, for instance, who have built a magical garden, like something from the Mediterranean, inside the foundation of a large old barn near Durham; or their neighbour John Bruce, who has built a vegetable garden walled with ruins from the local wreckers and constructed a tower from the

Dordogne (made with local granite) to overlook it and the wonderful rolling terrain of Grey County. We give one another plants . . . and ideas: the friendly Olympics of horticulture. It is as much pleasure to feel that I have given Georg and Karen the idea that all of their landscape (a much more dramatic landscape than mine) should be congruent with the experience of the garden as to know they have given me new ways of thinking about my pond and what might grow there.

One of the things that flourished there for the first time that summer was ducks: Muscovies that I had bought from the local farmers' market. They're the only ducks that will grow to any size in one summer, and I thought moreover (rightly, in the event) that they would keep down the duckweed in the pond. What a strange life they must have led there, somewhere between wild and tame: fed and yet free to wander . . . until, that is, it was September and time for the freezer.

The territory between wild and tame is as interesting as the overlap between art and nature. Now that my red squirrels are threatened by the invasion of the larger black ones, I feel more kindly towards them, the threatened species in my Amazonian rain forest. And now that the groundhogs have (largely) moved downhill from the house, I feel less inclined to get out my gun in the spring. Recently I have been adopted by a cat, a female tabby whom I call "Madam" because of her imperious demands for food. There have always been feral cats in the barn;

indeed, "Madam" was almost immediately hustled into a haymow by the black tomcat that lives in the barn when she first appeared. And now there are six cats where a few months ago there was only one. Madam seemed very tame: someone's pussycat thrown out of a car, I suspect. But one day when I picked her up in the house too abruptly, she sank her teeth savagely into my hand.

One of the lessons of the garden and landscape, then, is how to keep one's distance, to resist the temptation of possessive absolutism or Disneyfied cuteness. It is not a lesson that comes easily to the domineering geometric inclinations of the patriarchal mind, but it was one I was beginning to learn: a nurturing that was not mere control, a willingness to accept the seasons and to take opportunity as it served.

CHAPTER 9

ALL DIRT AND CONFUSION
POTTING SHEDS AND GARDEN ROOMS

Sometime in February 1992, Tim arrived at Stonyground one morning, asking if I had noticed the trees in the orchard. They had been protected with wrap-around tree-protectors, but this was a particularly ferocious winter and the snow was especially high. It turned out that in the space of one night a jackrabbit (I had seen him around) had completely girdled half of the new orchard, girdled the trees past the possibility of graft repair, that is. And by the time I had surveyed the rest of the trees on the place (the maples had never had protectors), I realized that more than sixty trees would have to be replaced. Tim was to spend a good part of the summer putting four-foot-high sections of white plastic drainage tile around the new trees; 'barn-door surgery', it might have been called.

Is there anything more dispiriting than having to start all

over again on a project of this magnitude? I had had one such set-back already, with the pines, but this was even worse. No visitor to the garden ever believes that nature is anything but benign, though many of them seem to forget that cancer and AIDS are part of "nature's way" too. Gardeners know better; they know the brassy triumphs of today may be cancelled by the sure obliterations of tomorrow: an uncontainable plague of earwigs, an unnoticed mould, the wind that slaughters the new-blown delphiniums and leaves the garden a tangled wreckage. "Gardeners," as the writer Harry Mitchell says, "are the ones who ruin after ruin get on with the high defiance of nature herself, creating, in the very face of her chaos and tornado, the bower of roses and the pride of irises."

The depredations of our friend the bunny were an augury of the worst year for weather yet, a year (thanks probably to the eruption of Mount Pinatubo) in which we had a severe frost in late May, and because of the constant rain my cousins would not get the soybean crop off the fields until December. I resolved to give up the unequal struggle with the wildlife and to fence the *potager* at last. I also resolved to get a rifle, though at that point I had more need of a shovel.

Fortunately not all of the season was like that. There was time in the spring, in the midst of the usual conifer planting, to make a wild garden down the wooded part of the hill in front of the house. From my cousin's woods my friend Ken Mews (another keen gardener) and I gathered white and red trilliums and hepaticas and leeks and wild ginger and Jack-in-the-pulpit and planted them into an almost identical habitat. Among them we scattered some of the daffodils that I dug up at my great-uncle's farm up the road, where they had run wild into the roadside. Through all of this wound down that part of the hill a new path and set of steps made from the closely sliced log of one of the old spruces that had had to be cut down.

The early hepaticas in my wild garden are shy comers; one needs to know to look for them, their delicate pink blooms hiding coyly under the apparently dead leaves of last year's plant. But the trilliums and the daffodils (which now spread across even more of the hill) make a cheerful splash, even at a time when spring seems not quite to have decided whether the whole business is a good idea or not. The kitchen window looks out on all this and down the hill, through two statuesque alders, to the pond, which at this time of the year beckons with a mountain-lake freshness. Over the window hangs a British Rail sign from some commuter station. Meant to separate the regular ticketholder from the occasional traveller, it says simply: "Seasons". It seemed the right text for the view from this window.

One of my colleagues insists that a wild garden is a contradiction in terms. It is an old debate, but one that had its highest profile in the late nineteenth century, when Reginald Blomfield sparred it out with William Robinson. Robinson, the great exponent of the wild garden, was in fact attacking the carpet-bed horrors of Victorian planting of annuals: the sort of thing made possible by the spread of greenhouses in the wake of the abolition of the window tax. But the argument remains a real one, one situated in the larger art versus nature debate that never really gets solved and that Michael Pollan has taken on so wittily in his book, *Second Nature*. What is wild or tame depends upon your definitions of both terms. Money plant and sweet rocket are the "wild" flowers on that hill, but they are exotic imports, now naturalized, while the trilliums and Jacks-in-the pulpit are native. Now the tame-gone-wild has to be weeded out so that expelled wild flowers may be returned to their habitat!

Here, then, was another treaty between the tame and the wild, like the intervention in the grove on the eastern walk, where the war with Canada thistles and woody nightshade seemed best dealt with, first by herbicide and then by wood chips on the path and central clearing. Left to itself, nothing we had planted in the grove could survive the onslaught of these marauders, most of them exotic introductions that followed the clearance of the land.

I have no intention of trying to roll back the clock to 1850: the date of European settlement here. One could not do that if one wanted to. The flora that was cleared then was arboreal; the landscape we have now is largely the agriculture of tillage. Even were we to "let the land go back", what would take over (for most of a lifetime) would not be the pre–1850 woodland plants, but the rampant invaders that we have introduced, the wild flower–weeds that thrive on our agricultural margins. Even a vigorous program of replanting trees will not, and cannot, exactly reproduce the world of the old forests. The spectacular forest horizons of Amy and Claire Stewart's garden in Caledon, north of Toronto, are a combination of existing old forest and new coniferous planting. But they are spectacular because the trees were brushed on with a painter's eye, a painter aware of the way in which all these elements (including the constructed ponds at the landscape's centre) make a composition that we now (thanks to the landscape painters of the Canadian Shield) think of as "natural".

Nature, in spite of what landscape calendars suggest to the contrary, is not a fixity. The shrubbery that we think ideal grows into a tangled mass; the tree that seems just the focus for the view grows up and obscures it. Even the distant woods (as I know) begins to come to the end of its cycle of growth. Ought one to intervene? Should the timber be harvested or left messily to rot?

Why did the introduction of black-eyed Susan into the garden prove a bad idea when the introduction of mallow was not? Why do I not mind the wild clematis growing its old-man's-beard through the elder at the compost yard when I resent its intrusions elsewhere? And why are echinops and eryngium (both of them thistles) acceptable cultivars in a garden when other thistles are not?

Curiously, this was also the summer that I discovered *Onopordum acanthium* (the real Scotch thistle) growing on the old railway bed. Railways are great spreaders of foreign plants, and this must have been one of them, for *Onopordum* was nowhere else to be found in the neighbourhood. Anyone who has been to a large English garden has seen it, but perhaps without recognizing it as a thistle. Like the artichoke, its size conceals its real nature from North Americans, who think of thistles as weeds no higher than a couple of feet. *Onopordum* is gigantic, and handsome standing in the back of a border. What's more, it is nothing like the spreader that most thistles are. So into the rose bed by the barn it went, and there it has prospered ever since, to the envy of many.

This, too, was the spring to deal with the problem of the red currants. Down by the road, some four hundred feet away and on the other side of the prevailing wind, they no longer seemed a danger to the pines, but they were quickly swallowed up in ferocious couch grass and bore but little fruit. It seemed time to give them a better home, a bed to themselves. Next to the lane below the orchard, my cousin tilled a bed fifty feet long with the cultivator and dug in manure. Into it went the red currants and some decorative roses; a big crop of berries (even after the birds have had their fill) has been the reward ever since.

But something major was happening while all this was going on. The pipe-dream of the previous year about what might be done with the back of the house had been handed to an architect, and the result was that the old summer kitchen was to be gutted completely and rebuilt as a garden room. And onto it, as a further extension of the house's "tail", was to go a further room to extend the house into the garden. As Jane Austen puts it in *Mansfield Park*, I was in for "three months of dirt and confusion", but it would be worth it.

As I have said already, nothing on the site was square to anything else: a truth all too obvious in the first aerial photograph of the gardens. Why *would* it have been? The buildings had been constructed where they best suited the site; the amazing thing is that they were in any alignment at all. The new gardens had been "fudged" with the edges of the hedge-on-sticks, to look as if they were square to both the house and the barn. It was now the house's turn to make some response.

My initial notion had been simply to put French doors in the back wall of the old house. "You've not thought about this," said my martinettish architect. "The back wall of the house belongs to the garden, not the house." And he was right: I hadn't thought enough about it. After much toing and froing I was to be much further in debt, but much happier with the result. There would be an eight-foot window in the old summer kitchen from which one could see into the garden, even from the interior of the house. And, even more forcefully, there was to be a gothic window in the new room (a copy of some of the old windows in the main block of the house) that would look down the hedge-on-sticks and bring the house at last into axis with the spine of the gardens.

The new room, sitting just where the old maple had

been, was to have skylights and French doors as well. In the summer it would be a dining-room, so that it would seem as if one were eating in the garden but free from mosquitoes: no mean consideration that wet year. But its true function was as a growing house for plants, a place where they could be started in flats on the heated stone floors in March, then be lifted up on trestles to the skylights, and finally be taken into the *potager* in May. And so it was called "the potting shed".

Here, then, was the house going out to greet the garden, even in all weathers. For there was to be a large fireplace in the redone back kitchen (now "the garden room"): a fireplace known as a Rumford, after the American who had discovered in the late eighteenth century that a shallow fireplace with a proper draught casts more heat into the room than a conventional one. And outside, backing onto that fireplace and its new-built chimney, was to be a barbecue big enough to roast a side of lamb, adjacent to the new terrace, rebuilt from the pathetic thing that I had constructed behind the house.

All of this building had begun in February, and by the end of June it was virtually complete. The tulips I had planted behind the construction site managed miraculously to survive, and to them I added alliums and hostas: a sweep of colour and foliage out towards the pump-house and the Great Garden, which were now part of the distant view.

It was in 1992, as well, that I began to reconfigure the other bed behind the house: the large area between the path to the *potager* and the path to the pump-house. An earlier path, constructed there from the back of the house, had been removed, but there was a legacy of heavy gravel to deal with and new planting to be done. I decided to sow it with small bulbs (mostly *Fritillaria meleagris*) and to over-plant it with vinca.

Vinca grows wild by many of the roadsides in the country, its charming blue flower a legacy of lost homesteads (like lilac and orange day lilies). Near me was such a road-side, and so I helped myself. Mistake! Well, not the vinca, but my carelessness in not checking to see that among its many roots was not concealed the villain couch grass. I have since redug that garden twice in an attempt to weed it . . . to no avail. Now, three years later, I have dug it again, this time to remove the vinca and lamium (cleansed of couch grass) to the new nursery, there to await a spring retransplantation *after* I have twice sprayed the whole area for couch grass. Having first reduced the number of trees there, I have underplanted now with more fritillarias, *Scilla campanulata*, and alliums. And next spring the centre will be replanted with hostas. No longer, I hope, the overgrown eyesore that my impatient enthusiasm first created, it will become a suitable vista from the house.

Into part of that vista in 1992 came two new installa-tions. One entailed the removal of the marten house from the herb garden to the pond, where there was more hope of the birds taking up residence. In its place went a sundial, another Tobey creation, carved on the four sides of its plinth with a text from Marvell's poem "The Garden" — "reckon'd but with herbs" — in the typeface of the first edition of his poems. The other new installation was the *ara pacis* that I have written about already: the peace monument by the sculptor Andy Drenters that answers the wind pendulum in the walk's forecourt, and terminates with its torquing ploughshare the view from the window in the potting shed down the long hedge-on-sticks walk.

Not all of this was building done without my part. The stone for the floors in the potting shed had to be fetched from Ledgerock Quarry, but while I was there I began to collect the materials for another long-speculated installation. Ledgerock had relatively recently begun to import Indiana limestone for turning and carving. (The local limestone is striated and unsuitable for working.) Many of their early experiments were failures, and there were several great piles of spoiled cornices and architraves and pillars: enough to set me thinking again about the monument to the earls of Elgin (after whose family, the Bruces, the county is named) that I had intended to make.

Bruce County had been named after the eighth earl, who was governor general at the time that the purchase (or do we say "theft" nowadays?) of the territory was made from the Ojibwa. He was the son of the man who had taken the so-called Elgin Marbles from the Parthenon in Athens: that wonderful set of sculptures of riders and horses, known as the "metopes", that are now in the British Museum in London.

Following in his footsteps, the eighth earl, having returned to England from Canada and been sent to China to
put down the Opium War, proceeded to avenge the deaths
of some British soldiers by destroying Yuan ming yuan. This
was the imperial palace known as the City of Heavenly
Peace that had been built in the eighteenth century under
the direction of Italian Jesuits.

It seemed a lot of ruin in two generations, and so a monument to their memory, with the "ruins" from Ledgerock,
seemed an appropriate commemoration. Columns, architraves, volutes, entablatures tumbled over an old stone pile.
And on to one of them, a piece shaped like a framed
entablature, Tobey carved the signature of the eighth earl: a
signature that I had copied from one of his letters in the
British Library.

That was not Tobey's last commission that year, for in
the woods there was a stone that also asked for an inscription. In one of my classes, a course in modern poetry, we
had studied the work of Lorine Niedecker, a Wisconsin
poet who had written a poem, "Lake Superior", about the
Jesuit explorer Marquette. "Through all this granite land,"
the poem read, "the sign of the cross". "What does this
mean?" I had asked the group, none of whom seemed ever
to have encountered the geology of the Shield. "Marquette
was founding missions," said one; "No, he was seeing
visions," said another. None of the students would credit
that granite could have a schist formation in it that looked
like a cross, and my saying there was such a stone in my

Detail of the Elgin monument near the woods

The herb garden and sundial inscribed with part of Marvell's "The Garden"

Opposite Looking across the Great Garden towards the Apollo
monument in late summer

woods did not persuade them. I got Lorine's signature from a poet friend who had been her correspondent, and Tobey signed the rock with it. It's an epitaph to the poet's close observation, and it requires a sharp eye to spot the signature on the walk through the woods.

That summer my cousins were much taken up with the preparations for the International Plowing Match which was to be held on their land in the autumn of 1993. Part of the preliminary clean-up involved dismantling a two-storey stone pigpen that our grandfather had built on one of their farms: a building that had been damaged in the tornado of 1969 and never used again. Some of its dressed stone came down to Stonyground, to be built into a wall next to the barn terrace two years later.

That was not the only instance of recycling. Near the *potager* the previous year we had cut down a walnut tree that was both shading and poisoning that garden. But none of the local sawmills was prepared to cut into timber the two eight-foot logs that had been saved from it . . . for fear that there might be wire buried in the tree that would destroy their saws. Finally I found a man near Durham with a portable band-saw who spent a long afternoon turning and manipulating those logs through the saw: a craftsman who was a wood-butcher in the best sense of that word, and a great pleasure to watch. Out of this milling came what my house carpenter said was about two thousand dollars' worth of lumber. Three years later, Tim has shaped the wood into an armoire — a magnificent scaled-down copy of an early Ontario piece — that looks out the window to the site of its former self.

These are not the exhilarating pleasures of the first interventions: the circle in the *potager* or the levelling of the Great Garden. But they are the more rewarding for being the result of congruency: the sense that one is at last in tune with what is there. As the garden comes to look as if it had always been there, one sees the thing that was missing or how something else can be placed. Best of all, perhaps, the garden becomes a place for all seasons, a place to be looked into on a summer morning awash with mist or on a winter one, when the first wet snow has dusted it like a Christmas card. It becomes a place, not just for doing, but for contemplation.

CHAPTER 10

THE CHINESE WAY
OF GARDENING
WILD AND TAME

In the summer of 1992 I had stocked the pond with trout:
a tricky operation that involved a high-speed transfer of the
trout from the hatchery in Hanover, ten miles away. After
an initial sluggish moment or two, they had taken to the
pond in style, and we had had several fine meals from
them. Now I hate fishing, but many of my friends do not.
And certainly I do not hate eating fish. Almost immediately, though, the attentive eye of the blue heron was upon
them. Grateful as I was to the herons for keeping down the
volume of the frog chorus (and I rather hoped the fish
would curtail the tadpoles too), I was apprehensive that I
would have no fish, in spite of their having lots of deep
water in which to avoid the heron.

Over that winter my friends George the bricklayer and his
partner, Susan the quilter, had made me a beautiful heron

decoy. Carved by George and painted by Susan, it came equipped with special long legs so that it could be put in the water in summer. As a "decoy" it would work in reverse, saying, in effect, to any passing heron: "This pond is already booked." In fact it has never gone down to the pond. It is too beautiful to risk being damaged, and so it presides quite gracefully (if a little menacingly) in the house.

The lake had been made without much thought of how the plant life would regenerate around it, and although I had planted yellow flag and cardinal flower by the edges and a combination of tamarack and larch on the sand-gravel banks, I was allowing the rest of the site to regenerate from the adjacent species — mostly poplar and alder.

This was the summer when I first realized how necessary some hydraulic system would be for the pond. Fed by underground springs, its level depended on the rainfall of the summer and the strength of those springs. And this was to be a dry summer, when, on top of everything else, the run-up to the Plowing Match meant that enormous amounts of water were being drawn off from the aquifers by the town well next door.

That well had already caused problems with local wells and ponds. As usual, it seems, the Ministry of Natural Resources had been resolutely unhelpful and accepted the town's claim that the water they were drawing was from a different level. It must have been one of the rarest cases in modern hydrology: water that does not seek its own level. It was a vivid demonstration to me, however, of why farmers do not bother with government ministries about most problems.

My well, fortunately, went down to the aquifer that also fed the town well, and so, for the purposes of the house at least, we were equal competitors. The level of the lake, however, sank and sank, and the fish became more and more sluggish, until one day I saw them floating one by one to the surface, martyrs to the lack of oxygen and the diminished water supply.

I came to see that some system of supplying water to keep the pond at a regular level (and oxygenated) was necessary for the fish. And I had long realized that they would not breed either if there was no riprap, no gravelly waterfall in which they could lay their eggs. Three years later, this remains a problem, and I am still fishless. But I know that the solution is to supply the pond from the well with a constant flow of water that enters the pond in a waterfall. Money, money! For the time being, I shall have to do without my own fresh fish, and I am reminded of my problem every autumn when I see the great shoals of enormous lake salmon thrashing their way to death in the pool below the dam at Paisley.

That spring, Susan also made for me a long-standing project: a set of stair treads fashioned of floor-cloth painted with the worst weeds in the garden. This was not the first floor-cloth to be made for the house. An earlier one had been painted for the kitchen containing the names of dogs associated with famous gardens of the past, each in a typeface appropriate to its era. It was surrounded with a border in which was the text that Pope had written for the collar of the dog he had given to the Prince of Wales: "I am his

Highness' dog at Kew, Pray tell me Sir whose dog are you?" In the midst were the horticultural dogs: Pope's dog, "Bounce", and her friend, "Fop", the dog of George II's mistress at nearby Marble Hill; John Evelyn's dog "Piccioli" in an appropriately Italianate script, as with "Signor Fido": another faithful Italian, as his elaborate monument among the British Worthies says at Stowe. Rousham, the home of "Ringwood", another dog celebrated by an elaborate monument, is in the Gothic style, and so is Ringwood's name on the mat. "Bruce and Bruno" were dogs at Erdigg, a garden that descended in the Lloyd family almost untouched into the twentieth century. And so they, like "Guy", my friend Allen Paterson's dog, have a plain modern typeface. I walk back and forth over them, but rather as I might a gravestone in a cathedral, with no disrespect.

The weed-treads, however, are another story: far more vindictively enjoyable. Carefully copied from botanical books, the weeds look pretty enough, but morning and evening (at least) one has the pleasure of grinding them under one's heel. Fourteen steps in all: if you know your weeds, you will also be able to spot that the whole infamous fourteen compose (roughly) the rhyme-scheme of a Shakespearean sonnet.

Dandelion
Burdock
Bladder Campion
Red Dock
Fleabane

Cinquefoil

Purslane

Horsetail

Milkweed

Couch Grass

Pigweed

Shepherd's Purse

Canada Thistle

Sow Thistle

There is a sonnet to cheer the weeder's heart as he plods wearily to bed.

Over the late winter and early spring, Tim had also been making an "installation" for me: a reproduction of the first chinoiserie building in England, the Chinese House at Stowe. Now neither of us had ever seen that building; indeed, not many had. It had been taken away from Stowe in the eighteenth century and had spent a good deal of its recent life in Ireland. What I knew about it was derived largely from a photograph in Patrick Conner's *Oriental Architecture in the West*: a book I had consulted for a lecture on the Chinese garden in England at a conference at the Royal Botanic Gardens the previous year.

I had kept ducks on the lake for two years, and this little building appeared to be an ideal duck house, although that seems not to have been its original use at Stowe. With the help of two willing students who came up to deal with the hill-meadow that spring, the building was loaded onto the truck and brought over from Tim's workshop. With a great deal of effort, it was manhandled onto the raft on the pond, but the first strong wind shifted it off (fortunately, into the shallow end of the pond), and a further manhandling was required to get it up to what is its final resting-place on the bank at the northern end. Now painted red and blue and yellow (though it has yet to get its final chinoiserie stencilling), it turns an unprepossessing pond into a startling vista, especially in winter, when its bright red can be seen from the road.

This was not the only "Chinese" acquisition of the spring. From the (alas defunct) store Re-Orient, in Toronto, I had bought several Chinese crocks: enormous rough-cast things that now punctuate the garden. As with the old maple-syrup pots that I had already, these and other planters serve to break the edges of the gardens and to step them down and out into the walks. Never filled with earth (they would be an impossible chore to empty in our sudden autumns), they have cunning false bottoms that turn them into no more than oversized flowerpots. Nonetheless, they look as if they are mini-versions of the garden squares, overflowing with flowers like fountains.

Already a number of local groups had come to see the garden, and it was becoming apparent to me that some provision would have to be made for parking so that the garden did not end up looking like a car park with some flowers attached. The field in front of the house had been planted as an orchard, but I had been warned by wise local heads

Chinese House by the lake

not to take the trees any closer than one hundred feet from the road because of the winter salt-spray. This left an odd bit of grassy meadow across the bottom of that field: a piece that seemed ideal as a car park as it was on very gravelly, well-drained land and close to the road.

I had also been having increasing trouble with dirt bikes and snowmobiles on the railway right-of-way. One neighbour had had his dog killed by one of them. The railway company showed no interest either in returning the land to me (it had been ceded for a railway after all, not a dirt-bike track) or in keeping up the fences. When I blocked off the right-of-way that separates the pond from the house, these town hooligans simply cut across my orchard, in the winter damaging the young fruit trees with their snowmobiles. The solution seemed to be to make a bed of rugosa roses all across the northern side of the new car park. Even snowmobiles and dirt bikes don't mess with those thorns. And so a bed of rugosas it was, with a carpet of sea-foam roses in front to cover the bed in another sort of lethal but pretty carpet. Now, two years later, it is large and lush, providing roses until well into the autumn, and leaving me to wonder why I bother with any other than rugosas.

That May I had a paper to give in Washington, and afterwards I went with my Dutch garden-historian friend round fifteen historic gardens in Virginia: a magical time when all sorts of garden ideas suggested themselves. One that came from Jefferson's endlessly inventive Monticello was the idea of using stake-and-rider rail fences, both for verticality in the garden and as supports for grapevines. On my return, one fence went down the back of the new rose border, another around the top of the berm on what will be the water garden in the gravel pit (to encourage the wild grape to grow up it), and a third for cultivated grapes along the west side of Gugliano, the outer vegetable garden.

Grapes take a long while here and are a chancy thing at best. Even the old Concords that I have trained onto the arbour are taking their own sweet time about making it the leafy paradise that I had hoped. The ferocity of our winters and the constant die back are difficult for most visitors to believe, even visitors from Toronto, where laburnum and wisteria will easily survive. At one time I had thought of planting the southwest-facing hill-meadow by the gravel pit with hardy grapes. Perhaps I still shall, if my energy holds up. Certainly it was encouraging to see what my friend Patrick Bermingham had done with interesting grapes on his south-facing slopes in Ancaster, near Hamilton. But that, as Allen Paterson often reminded me about the nearby Royal Botanical Gardens, is a considerably milder zone. Bruce County is not the Niagara Peninsula, nor known for its viticulture. One dreams, none-theless, of walking nonchalantly among the vines, a glass of one's own Chablis in hand!

Fortunately, as I have said, I have several devoted friends who seem to think that nothing is better than a weekend slaving with a shovel in the country. One of them is Dennis Findlay, the baker, and the builder of the set of railway-tie steps down the hill. In the summer of 1993 he reappeared one weekend to create a new bed. For some time I had been unhappy about a little strip of grass next to the car park on the north side. I'm not quite sure now why the car park hadn't simply taken it over, as the northern side of the grass strip was bordered by the little hedge of pines along the side of Barn Lawn. Perhaps it was that the car park was made to be square to the arbour, and here was a bit of ground parallel to the oval garden that lined up neither with one thing nor with another. But the real problem was that, as visitors arrived in the car park, there was nothing to "announce the garden", nothing, that is, to suggest what lay beyond the hedges that confronted them.

It was time to do something about that, especially since this was to be the first year of a tour from Toronto. The previous winter I had taught a course in garden history for a private group in North Toronto. It was my first venture outside the university and an augury of things to come as I began to think about how Stonyground might develop. The tour was coming: as ever, an occasion for a project.

But such projects are never as simple and straightforward as one imagines with one's winter doodlings. The soil on the site of that bed was gravelly trash and needed extensive improvement. Fortunately some thirty-year-old manure in the barn was just the ticket, but before we could get at that, some of the old horse stalls needed to be removed, revealing (as I suspected) that serious repairs would have to be done soon to the barn.

Making and planting the bed took more than a weekend,

but the real work, the back-breaking work, was done then. Dennis and I went after the old manure that, even after thirty years, had a ripe and overwhelming pong. There must have been nearly fifty barrowloads of it carted up to the site of the new bed by the car park and dug in. And into that bed went white tulips for early effect, followed by iris in a range of colours across the bed, then a diversity of day lilies, and finally phlox and hostas. Along the front, next to the car park, went a range of sedums. By the time it was finished, I had got my first load of perks from the Plowing Match: wood-chip mulch to keep down the weeds — a huge mound of it that went on the long border too, and even into the Great Garden. One has to be careful with that kind of mulch, for initially it drains the nitrogen from the soil, so additional fertilizer high in nitrogen needs be used — but wood-chip mulch is preferable to straw because it contains no weed seeds.

The previous year I had fenced the *potager* against nature's little (and big) ravishers, but this had left me with gates of fence wire that were both unattractive and awkward. The solution was to call in another local carpenter, Don Hehn, who had made the screen doors and bookshelves for the addition to the house and was now to make portals and gates for the entrances to the vegetable garden. These were made with white cedar, the local cedar that I had wanted to use for the pergola on the back of the house six years earlier. At that time there was no local cedar to be had in the market, not even for ready money. Now that red cedar from British Columbia was an outrageous price, it had become profitable

View out of the Great Garden through stumping harrow gate
to the transverse avenue

for local farmers to take out cedar logs, and what I had originally wanted then was now available.

It is a strange thing, this local lumber trade: a matter of
knowing who is likely to have what. The writer Clifford
Geertz called it "local knowledge", and so much a part of the
"scene" is it that no one imagines that a stranger or an out-
sider might not know it. Some of it was obscure even to my
cousins: what the Mennonites might have milled, for instance, or what sort of woodworking they might do. My dear
late friend Geoffrey and his wife, Judith (my earliest visitors),
had discovered that the Mennonites made garden swings —
the wonderful platform-rocker kind — and they had driven
themselves crazy trying to figure out how they might get one
back to New York.

It was not the Mennonites that Don went to in this
instance, but a local farmer he knew, and within a few weeks
he reappeared with twelve-foot uprights, gates, and the gull-
wing ornaments that are copied from the pergola. The gates
had to be wide enough to encompass four-foot walks and yet
not look awkward, but he had worked that one out too, and
the only real obstacle was the post-holes and the rocks that
lurked within them.

I left that to Tim and Don. That year my right arm had
started to "play up" — the result, it turned out, of a pinched
nerve in my neck: a problem that had more to do with cran-
ing over a computer screen than with gardening. I had to go
for therapy and do tedious exercises (I am very impatient of
any illness), and they had to get on with the gates. One of

the gates I could not decide how to position — the one that led into the garden from the hedge-on-sticks. It could not have a portal because of the hedge itself — at that point gradually being trimmed into a double arch. And so it too had to lie fallow until I realized, the following year, that a simple gate without a portal was not incongruous, and the obvious solution.

Fortunately I was not completely incapacitated. There were other projects to get on with, other inscriptions to be arranged. At the entrance to the *potager* went a single flagstone with some words from Virgil that had haunted me while I was working on my book on English planters. They were from his description in the fourth *Georgic* of the old man of Taranto whose vegetable garden provided all his sustenance. He needed to buy nothing, and so was the model of the agricultural utopia. "Unpurchased delicacies" was how Virgil described his garden, and so it seemed right that the old man of Toronto (me) should have "*dapes inemptae*" at the entrance to his vegetable garden too.

The far end of the *potager* was the site of the largest installation that year: a monument to Apollo to "answer" the stone to his sister Diana that stands east of the Great Garden. On one of my trips to Ledgerock Quarry, I had noticed a handsome limestone column lying in the stone-yard: a reject, it turned out, from a building project in Toronto. Ten feet tall, with a simple capital and base, it seemed to ask for a place in the garden, and I began to think how it might be used.

Tim and I talked about it, with the result that, for the top

Part of quotation from William Kent
in the main avenue to the woods

of the column, he made a great "sun": an iron circle surrounded by what look like giant arrowheads. Here was
Apollo's symbol, the sun, made with his arrows of destruction (actually the "guards" off an old binder). The final image
suggested the head of a dandelion: no inappropriate allusion,
in that Apollo was originally the same god as Priapus, the
insem-inator, and no plant is a greater inseminator than the
dandelion.

One day in midsummer a great truck arrived with a crane,
and the driver, with a skill that is always a pleasure to watch,
manoeuvred the column down into the site we had prepared:
a paved recess in the elder hedge, just at the end of the transverse walk of the Great Garden and facing Diana, nearly two
hundred feet away. Onto its top went the gilded steel corona
of the sun: a construction that pivots on a pin set in the top of
the column. I was delighted to discover subsequently that the
prevailing northwest winds of early winter move the corona
to face southeast, as if it were a giant phototropic sunflower.
Later that year Tobey was to carve Apollo's other name,
"Priapus", into the column, but the inscription is in Greek so
as not to offend the tender sensibilities of garden-matrons!

But Apollo was not to be the only inscribed monument
that year. Ever since the Kent–Hogarth installation, I had wanted to include Kent's famous dictum "Nature abhors a straight
line." That summer Tobey carved it — one letter per one-
foot-square flag of limestone. It was designed to go in the
main avenue (a dead straight path), each square separated from
the next by three feet of grass. Thus the walker would have to

compose a text in his mind that rebuked the actions of his feet. And so it is, though I may have to complement it with one of the many natural forms in our landscape that do have straight lines: a rock with a straight fissure, perhaps, and on it Kent's name in a circle, cancelled with the line of the fissure.

That summer the walker would probably have been heading for the woods, where by now there were a number of inscriptions. At the entrance to the woods: the Dante inscription done in the first year facing the Palmer bird-box and the Rackham beech; the Marvell "Corinthian Porticos" in another bird–box announcing the soaring maples of the walk in terms of the architectural forms derived from them; the Niedecker stone almost hidden from the walk; the Traherne warning about Satan in the darkest part of the woods.

That part of the woods, in other words, was becoming an associative walk, and there was a new fortuitous association. That year a pair of beaver began to make a dam, and although I never saw those shy creatures, their handiwork was obvious enough. It set me thinking about the rest of the woods and about other paths (and perhaps even ponds) that I had not thought about since the earliest days. And so the next year's project began to take shape in my mind: a path through the woods near the stream that would be a return to my initial plans.

The main avenue to the woods

CHAPTER 11

Look up to Woods

Bridges, Walks, and Paths

The tenth anniversary of the garden in 1994 was to be the first year when outside attention was focused on it in any significant way. That June came busloads of visitors from Toronto, fortunately on idyllic days. Indeed it was an idyllic summer altogether. The horrific winter (that I had missed by being on sabbatical in England) had as its corollary a summer of unparalleled fecundity. And I, having had the daffodils in late January in London, had the pleasure of having them twice over as the spring at Stonyground was late.

By the time I returned at the beginning of May, the seedlings that Susan had started in the potting shed were robust and eager for the garden. But it was still far too early for that, and I was still examining the winter casualties. The wisteria that ought not to have been hardy here in the first place had been planted in the most sheltered spot on the east side of the house and had prospered there. But it looked as if it had perished along with the even hardier Dutchman's pipe. Neither had, it turned out, but this was to be a season for noting losses and taking what cheer I could from Harry Mitchell's definition of the gardener as one who persists in the teeth of such things.

Because the spring was slow, the bulbs lasted longer than usual. So often the late tulips and peonies bloom and die together in a sudden blaze of unseasonal heat. The slow season also meant that things were less frenetic in the garden. Tim came early in April, and we were able to keep ahead of most of the urgent tasks; for once, the *potager* was well prepared long before the vegetable seedlings were ready to go out.

The back of the house, where the new rooms are, was never originally meant as an entrance, but increasingly (especially in the bad weather) the potting shed became a sort of mud room/decompression chamber on the way in from the garden. And many visitors took to coming in that way too, so that the original paths on that side of the house seemed mean and insufficient. One of the late-spring tasks was to widen the paths and to give that side of the house some sense of occasion.

In the process I got rid of the first herb garden, which had largely been overtaken by lemon balm and chives: two ferocious spreaders. There's only so much of either that one is likely to want, though I had taken to making a quite successful chive vinegar. (Fill a gallon jug as tightly as you can with the chive blossom; add white vinegar until the jug is full; wait until it is pink. A delicious subtlety!) So the chives went out to the walnut hedgerow by "Brian's Walk", and the lemon balm went (largely) into the compost before it got to seeding itself again.

The bed next to the terrace on that side had also seemed inconsequential: a place for the porcelain berry that now runs all over the pergola to root itself, with a floral covering of this and that, and a hedge of hollyhocks, to give a sense of enclosure to the terrace. As much of the bed was gravelly debris, the answer seemed to be to expand and improve it with compost. With the coming into its own of the cedar hedge to the west, that area of the garden too began to acquire a sort of garden-room privacy and a character of its own: an increasing necessity if the garden was to be open more of the time.

It is difficult to exaggerate the effect of hedges and walls in gardens, especially large gardens. But walls are expensive, and have to be carefully made in our climate. George had found, to his chagrin, that the curved wall had begun to "spald" (shale off in layers) because of the damp and the sub-zero cold. The top had to be removed that year and a layer of protective felt put in before the bricks at the top of the wall were replaced. Hedges are cheaper. Not indestructible, they nonetheless make more handsome and comfortable enclosures once they are established. Sometimes, especially to the northern gardener, that seems a long "once", but then one year one realizes with a pleasant surprise that the trees have come into their own and are actually keeping the snow and the wind at bay.

At the end of June I went off to England for a couple of weeks and came back to find that Tim had already begun the path in the eastern cedar woods that we had talked about earlier. I had long wanted to make a path in this re-growth woodland: a path that would meander down to the stream there and connect with a long arcade of columnar cedars that grew on the north side of the stream. These in turn would lead back to the original path in the woods: the "Huron Road" that we had carved out through the decid-uous woods to make the perimeter-path connections in 1985.

And so it was: a chain-saw and a brush-eater, some path-making over swampy bits . . . and suddenly (it took only a few days) a whole new kind of woodland experience. My namesake, the eighteenth-century landscaper and architect Sir William Chambers, the maker of the gardens at Kew, believed in the "Chinese" pleasures of gloomy woods. These woods are not particularly gloomy, though they are somewhat mysterious, and I was delighted to find in the process of making this path that I owned a large area of young cedars of which I had been unaware. These two or three acres, populated largely by deer, seemed an ideal place for a hermitage: a retreat for visitors who wanted to get away to read and write, or even just to get away. I'm not sure yet just what form this "hermitage" will take: largely a screened-in pavilion, I would think, but it is a nice speculation for idle moments. And the whole of that woodland walk was part of the gathering-in of the landscape to the larger plea-sure of the *ferme ornée*.

Cedar walk in the woods by the stream

Another speculation began to take shape that summer. I had come back from England with Andy Goldsworthy's new book, *Stone*. For years Goldsworthy, a Scot, had been creating installations of great loveliness out of leaves and grasses and snow; but all of them were transitory monuments for the camera alone. Now he was working in stone and had, indeed, made a huge cairn in Illinois out of granite glacial till.

Here was what I had been looking for: something that would serve as a punctuation for the view from the gardens towards the woods. "Look up to woods and down to water" was the motto of the eighteenth-century designer. I needed something to focus the eye on the woods, a giant piece of "punctuation" that said, in effect, "Look here!" And, also in the best eighteenth-century manner, it would invite the walker into the landscape but forbid walking to it directly. What the eye travelled to directly, the feet would have to approach more circuitously, and in the process discover other vistas, not least the vista back to where the eye had started. And so it was begun, and here is a project for the tractor when the farm does not demand it, a project that will take some years to complete, probably. The one sure thing is that there is no dearth of stone!

One of those stones finally came into its own this year: a handsome piece of veined pink granite that had turned up among the rubble of the pigpen. Shaped vaguely like a harp, it put me in mind of a text that I had wanted to incorporate on the western walk: an area particularly deficient in installations. There, just where there is a bridge over the medial stream in the fields, I had planted in the second year a weeping willow. In fact, I had planted two, but one of them had turned up its toes.

Now that tree was twenty feet tall, and its Latin name — *Salix babylonica* — suggested the biblical text that had, I assume, originally given it its name. Based on the dubious assumption that the trees of Babylon were willows, the botanists of the sixteenth century named this one for the Hebrew psalm of exile:

> *By the waters of Babylon we sat down and wept: when we remembered thee, O Sion.*
> *As for our harps, we hanged them up: upon the trees that are therein.*

Tobey suggested a Babylonish cuneiform script, and the word "Harps" was duly inscribed on this vaguely harp-shaped stone: a kind of mute singing about a song that could not be sung but has given its song to a tree.

This water-garden part of the walk still needs more work, and perhaps some weirs to give it another sort of melody. One landscape-architect friend has offered to make a bench for me, and I would like to place it near this stream, where the music of the water might be heard even on dry summer evenings: an auditory complement to the delicious watercress that grows there and graces our salads.

Just beyond the stream the walk now joins the old rail-way right-of-way, and one can choose to walk on grass (the old path by the hedgerow) or walk through onto a firmer and straighter path (the railway bed). This making of choices was a feature of William Kent's early eighteenth-century garden at Rousham, where the choice of paths to be fol-lowed was ostensibly between one that led to love (Venus) and another that led to wisdom (Apollo). The recent dis-covery that the statue of Apollo is actually of Antinous, the lover of the Emperor Hadrian, however, may give the choice between him and Venus a different meaning.

This was the year when another eighteenth-century installation came closer to being realized as well. I had at long last got to know Patrick Bermingham, a painter and sculptor who happens also to be an engineer and who had been a friend of Peter Day's. It was Patrick whom Peter had approached in 1989 about doing a homage to Capability Brown in this landscape: an installation based on a famous conversation that Brown had had with the bluestocking writer Hannah More. Responding to her question about how he made his landscapes, Brown had given her a lec-ture that she reported in a letter to her sister:

> *"Now there," said he, pointing his finger, "I make a comma, and there," pointing to another spot, "where a more decided turn is proper, I make a colon; at another part, where an inter-ruption is desireable to break the view, a parenthesis; now a full stop, and then I begin another subject."*

Peter's idea was to create a series of seats made of concrete and scatter them around the perimeter walk: seats composed of colossal commas, periods, and parentheses. When the estimate for the first parenthesis came in at fifteen thousand dollars, I abandoned hope. Now here was Patrick, at last on the scene, offering to make at least one of the parentheses of sheet steel as a memorial to Peter. And I had just the place for it: a nice view about two-thirds of the way down the eastern walk, where one looks out into the borrowed landscape of my neighbours' fields and woods, and parenthetically captures them into my landscape.

That walk, bordered with an interesting hedgerow of mountain-ash, wild cherry, and apple, and lined on the other side with transplanted maples, was just coming into its own at last, thanks not least to my having made an arrangement with my mechanic neighbour to rent his riding mower. What had been coarse-cut was now trimmed, though the grass was no Kentucky Blue. Starting for most walkers at the transverse avenue, the walk was announced by another new (though temporary) installation. On the site of what would be the Temple of Ceres, I had set up a plough brought to me by my cousin: one of the many items that had had to be cleared out of his farm the previous year to make way for the International Plowing Match.

This was not any old plough, but the first two-furrow plough to be used on any of the family farms. It had belonged to my great-uncle Lorne, a bachelor who had escaped from this farm to "go west", been wiped out by grasshoppers in his first year in Alberta, and returned to run his own one hundred acres up the road, known ever after as "The Ranch". A man of solitary though cheerful habits, he was also my first encounter with epilepsy: a disease that half a century ago was still thought to have been caused by some moral failing — in his case, an overfondness for his niece. One of the early horrors of my life was coming upon him in the lane to the barn at my grandmother's, where he lived, lying full-length, foaming at the mouth, the milk pail spilled, and running away.

Usually, after milking, if I had done nothing to annoy him, he would let me walk beside him up the powdery gravel road in the dark to his barn, where he would then milk his own cows. They were said to be "wild", unused to strangers, so I would have to sit in some dark corner, watching him as the lantern went from cow to cow. A turtle cat followed him expectantly, hoping for him to squirt a teat into her mouth.

Milton describes hell as "darkness visible". It is a difficult concept for us to get our minds around, surrounded as we are everywhere (even in the country) with incident light. In the days before electricity, the night was black in an almost palpable way, and the stars intense in a way the Persians understood but we have lost.

Well, it was Lorne's two-furrow plough: a doubly charged implement, in that his brother, who had reigned at Stonyground, would have none of such newfangledness. To the end of his days, when my great-uncle Angus ploughed he did so as the Egyptians had, following an ox or a horse. To my astonishment I was to encounter someone else that year, a local man who came to one of my talks about Stonyground, who had ploughed forty acres as a boy with a single-furrow plough.

Most people think of the agricultural revolution as having happened in the eighteenth century: something associated with Jethro Tull and the seed-drill. But a far greater revolution has happened in the twentieth. A man who began life, like the ancient Egyptians, behind a single-furrow plough has lived to see what would take him the better part of a week done in a few hours by massive machinery.

"Jethro Tull" is a joke name to city-dewllers, but in fact he was no yokel. Educated at Oxford and the law courts, he carried on a spirited fight about the true meaning of Virgil's *Georgics* with the martinet of eighteenth-century garden theory, Stephen Switzer. Tull had his own ideas about what mythology meant too, and one of them was that the wrestling between Hercules and Antaeus, the giant of earth, was an allegory of ploughing. So up went the plough on a steel-beam plinth, and on it in letters of cut steel (and in a typeface appropriate to old farm machinery) the name "Hercules".

That eastern walk leads first to the grove where Tobey had carved the memorial stone to my mother, with its emblematic marguerite. This summer he added to it another inscription, on a half-column from Ledgerock, the word Ilium. It was for my aunt, my mother's favourite sister, and probably the greatest influence on my life: certainly the reason that I am a professor of English today. It seemed right that she should be near my mother, and that she, who had thought of the ancients as her contemporaries, should have "*Illium*" as her text. "Is this the face that launched a thousand ships and burnt the topless towers of Ilium," says Christopher Marlowe's Dr. Faustus when he sees Helen of Troy. My teacher-aunt was called "Helen".

Beyond the grove the eastern walk passes by the parenthesis site and comes finally to the Elgin memorial, just before the new path wanders off down into the cedar woods. By the summer of 1994 that monument was coming into its own: wild grape was growing over it gracefully and more "ruins" had been added. As usual they were the perks that came from a trip to Ledgerock, this time to get a plinth for a bird-bath in the garden. But there had been other "trouves" as well: in the midst of a surprising heap of old bits, a fine sandstone carving with the word *Albert*. It seemed a fitting complement to a Victorian house, so I bore it away.

The best, however, was a recently carved bit of foliage in a nice sandstone block: part, it seemed, of an aborted project for the Parliament Buildings in Toronto. The stone-carver had intended it, apparently, as a modern interpretation of the historical foliage on that building: appropriate, he thought, to the very modern head of the restoration architect of the project who had included himself in the "restoration".

Greek krater birdbath and plinth near the house

The great Victorian critic John Ruskin had insisted in his classic book *The Stones of Venice* that stone-carvers be allowed their own inventions. Indeed, this was the principle followed in the carving of that very Ruskinian building, University College, only a few hundred yards away from the Parliament Buildings. But such was not to be in this restoration. The foliage was cut out, and more "historic" foliage substituted. Good news for me! The original now supports an urn in the garden at Stonyground.

This urn was on the edge of an area that was about to be transformed that summer: the area west of the barn surrounding the barn ramp and beyond the rose garden. The major project for the year was the repair of the barn. Replacing the supporting timbers in the first year was, it turned out, only a temporary measure. The whole of the east wall of the stable was leaning out more and more each year and needed to be seen to. Nothing short of radical surgery would do.

Early in August the contractors finally arrived, to an accompaniment of whining saws, digging machines, gravel trucks, and concrete-pouring. Up on jacks went the part of the barn adjacent to the east wall, and over (alarmingly), with the push of a hand, went the old concrete walls, which rested on no foundation.

I had already begun to build a terrace on the other side of the barn: the terminus to the hedge-on-sticks walk that that path increasingly seemed to call for. This project had involved clearing out of the foundation of a long-departed drive shed a collection of weedy maples and some old agricultural rubbish so that a proper foundation of rock and gravel could be dumped within what was left of the old walls. Because the north wall of the foundation had largely disappeared, however, some substitute buttressing was necessary. And what better than the great concrete slabs of the east wall, which, thanks to the intelligent agility of another local contractor, were put carefully into place?

Even before all this digging and destruction, however, I had determined to rescue two wild old dog-roses that had grown up next to the east wall of the barn. Also the ancient rose of Chaucer's prioress, Madame Eglantyne, these two in the barnyard deserved a better fate than a backhoe. What's more, they belonged with their siblings, the other old shrub roses that grew in the rose garden west of the barn. In came the redoubtable John Deere bucket again, and out they went to a new home.

Well, of course, it's never as easy as that, is it? First there had to be a new bed, or perhaps two new beds (they're large roses), and then there had to be walls to the beds, and then there had to be steps between the walls, and then, and then . . . I spent two weeks making the steps at the end of the hedge-on-sticks: steps behind the Peace Monument that take the walker up onto the barn ramp, and so across to the new terrace site. They were made, not with the finished limestone flags that Ledgerock could provide, but with the flat limestone that turns up in the fields, part of the substrate that no stone-picker will ever exhaust.

My plan was for a set of what I call "The Lutyens Steps": the sort that the great English architect Edwin Lutyens commonly made in the gardens where he worked with Gertrude Jekyll. Lutyens, however, worked with finished stone! Two convex steps leading to a circular platform, and then two concave: it all seemed perfectly straightforward. Nothing is straightforward when you work with fieldstone. My steps, after much back-breaking work with a level, are at least more or less even, but I call them now "The Wells Steps", after that wonderful set leading up to the Chapter House in Wells Cathedral in England, worn over the centuries with passing feet, and waving like the sea!

These steps, spreading out to a quarter-circle as they descend, serve to connect the hedge-on-sticks walk with the path through the *potager*, now made and continued to enclose the rose bed with an angle: the hard edge on that side that it had long needed. And then there was the business of making the beds for the dog-roses, and before that the barn wall that backed one of them to point. Then the walls: local limestone again, but this time the rather more workable square chunks that make walls so hospitable to sedums. And in went some congenial phlox and chelone. Well, we shall see.

As this previously untouched area (an area not originally conceived of as part of the garden) proceeded, I began, like Brown, to see its capabilities. At the bottom of the barn ramp was a stone pile, the legacy of what had been bulldozed out of the way to make the nursery and the rose garden. Long the haunt of an ineradicable groundhog, this stone pile had resisted any attempt to grow anything over it. Even artemisia would not prosper there. Now there was a place for it, and into the waiting foundation (without the groundhog) the stones went. What was left was bulldozed down the slope to make a gentler approach to the barn than the sudden right turn that the tractors had had to negotiate previously.

But I do not remember being conscious that there had ever been a slope there, certainly not the drop to the field that I now could see. Next to the departed stone pile were two old maple trees, the trees that had born the brunt of the 1969 tornado and so saved the barn. Handsome again, they seemed to merit something better: a place for a prospect out over the fields, a bench perhaps. And then I realized that, because of the drop in elevation to the field, this was the place for the long-desired ha-ha: that cunning eighteenth-century device to make the garden seem contiguous with the fields by hiding a wall in what amounts to a ditch. What better use for those handsome squared stones from the demolished pigpen, and who better to effect it than Campbell and his bucket? Within two hours there was a wall three feet high and thirty feet long.

A day or two later, after much raking and levelling, the maples had the beginnings of a lawn under them. But what was this? A set of old harrows left to lean against one of them had been grown over by the tree. What should have been a nuisance was a find. Tim, who had already made one set of gates to the garden with some other harrows had, that summer, made a second set of gates from another Plowing Match cast-off. Even older than the first set, these "stumping harrows", as they were called, had been used in the first stump-filled fields after settlement. Made of iron-wood and medieval-looking spikes, they looked their ancestry, for they can be seen in the illumination for October in the *Très Riches Heures of Jean, Duc de Berry* and their lineage can be traced to the Romans. Mine hang now, looking barbaric and faintly Japanese, at the entrance from the Great Garden into Barn Lawn, in an arch made using the equally savage-looking teeth from an old hayloader.

Here, then, under these maples, this third set of arrows offered an invitation to another agricultural metamorphosis. What was it that was nagging at the back of my mind about this site? And then it came. Here was just the location that Gainsborough had used in his painting *Mr. and Mrs. Andrews:* under a tree by a grainfield, looking downhill. Tim has only begun to think about the bench project, but some old cultivators that came out of Campbell's swamp the previous year looked like good candidates. Mrs. Andrews's blue hoop skirt and her husband's gun may prove more problematic!

On the far side of this site, beyond the terrace-to-be and over the concrete-wall abutment, I had had moved a load of vermiculated limestone that Campbell had assembled for me several years earlier. It had been serving to keep the cars in the car park discreetly back and hidden by the curved wall. Now these stones could come into their own. Over the concrete went a load of good topsoil, and over that the vermiculated limestone, to form the rockery.

The soil had come from a berm at the east end of the barnyard, a berm largely composed of the junk originally shoved off Barn Lawn. It too had become groundhog heaven, so it was a special pleasure to have it removed and dumped along the north side of the barn, once the old stone piles there (more groundhog condos) had been dumped into the terrace foundation. And there, next season, would be the beginnings of a bed for cut and dried flowers: part of the first tentative steps towards Stonyground as a commercial and educational enterprise.

At the end of a season of building and pathmaking, it was good to dwindle down into a long gentle autumn. There were the bulbs to plant as usual, but not (for once) in an October snowstorm. In the *potager* the cabbage and kale lingered with the leeks, and even some resolute spinach. Slowly during the clean-up of the garden — the mowing of the perennials, the raking of the leaves — we ate our way through heavy soups and hearty stir-fries towards the first snow.

And what a snow it was, one day in early November, wet and clinging to everything, clinging to the harrow gates and the leafless hedge-on-sticks and the tall shrub-roses, like a magical reblooming: confirmation indeed of what Allen Paterson had said to me long ago about structure and mass in the garden. But, appropriate to a year of work on the peripheries, the walks through the woods were even better: improbable operatic sets lush with the silence of another season. The close of the year could not have been orchestrated better.

Afterword

Once after an unhappy and messy break-up with a lover, I wrote a poem called "Notes for Next Time". It would not be a bad text for a garden-maker. But second thoughts are the privilege of the smug, and I think perhaps I have learned as much from my mistakes as from my successes. Some of the ostensible successes turn out to be a curse.

I listen to professional gardeners on the CBC or the BBC and find myself increasingly annoyed by their complacent assurance about how things should be done, their priestly expertise. How do *they* know what my garden is like — its mix of loamy soil and gravelly subsoil, its killing northwest winds and its late frosts, and which are its most invasive weeds? The thin-lipped nanny is never far away from their advice: "Well, if you will refuse to turn your compost, dear, you know what will happen!" What about the thousand and one things that demand to be attended to long before compost-turning gets a look-in? No, it is largely a matter of finding out for oneself, I'm afraid, and of discovering others (preferably local) who are engaged in similar mad projects.

And so my projects go on, receding like the green light at the end of Daisy's dock in *The Great Gatsby* into a future of ever-greater insolvency. Some of them are big: the two temples, for example — of Ceres in the transverse avenue, and another to Aeolus, the god of the wind, in the spinney. Lesser ones too: the oft-put-off memorial to the departed railway, for example, that would consist of a set of the railway's debris. This would be a sort of rostral column of triumph in the Roman manner: spikes, couplings, clamps, and the like, welded to bolts that would secure them to the remaining signal column.

And there would be another lesser railway monument — well, perhaps more a monument to the poet Edward Thomas, slaughtered almost on the last day of the First World War. It would be an invocation of his poem "Adlestrop" about a forgotten "halt" on a branch railway in Gloucestershire and would take the form of a little covered seat by the railway walk, a place for tired walkers, a place to contemplate the birdsong of Bruce County. Maybe somewhere down by the railway, too, there will be the long-desired beehive made to the design by Sir Christopher Wren: a "hive for the honey bee", as Yeats says, but full of the dreams of agricultural heaven that those reformers of the seventeenth century held dear.

Some ideas are even more far-fetched. One of them is a colossal mock-up near the woods of one of Barbara Hepworth's sculptures: two sets of squares pierced with circles on top of one another — aligned so that the upper ones pick up and frame the ploughshare of the Peace Monument as one looks down the hedge-on-sticks. Another is, and where in the landscape I do not yet know, Paul Nash's painting *Equivalent for the Megaliths* created in three dimensions: the Stonehenge of Stonyground.

In the wake of the first magazine article on the garden, Stonyground has been inundated with visitors: more than five hundred in three days at one point! Well, of course, people who are interested must come, but not, not ever, as an alternative to an auction sale or the beach or a round of miniature golf.

"Private faces in public places," the poet Auden wrote, "are nicer and brighter than public faces in private places." What this means in my case is that I want "understanders" in my garden, not just "spectators": people prepared to get out and kick the ball around themselves, not just sit in the stands, whose notion of gardening is not getting someone else to do it . . . or something on TV. I want visitors who have been there themselves, who will look carefully and ask questions. So often I find groups huddled in the *potager,* bewildered among vegetables they don't recognize (and won't ask about) but at least taking comfort from the fact that nothing will challenge them there to think about what a garden is . . . or might be.

Sometimes I ask my students if they have ever prepared an extensive and elaborate meal only to find their guests talking and arguing through it without noticing anything they're eating. It's the way many people read books, with half an ear on the TV. Europe is full of North Americans being dragged around art galleries, theatres, and historic sites: people who have never been to see a play, or looked at a painting, or even know whether the Greeks came before the Romans. What are they *seeing*, these culture-tourists? Do they expect art and civilization to fall upon them like grace, without even the imaginative equivalent of Christian repentance?

Several years ago I noticed that one of my students was wearing a T-shirt that read "Toronto the Fun University". It was a sign of the passive rot that infects a society that defines itself in terms of consumption. "Fun" in that sense means programmed amusement, the Disneyland of the mind: what Aldous Huxley meant by the word "soma" in *Brave New World*. It is the decreation of intelligence, and ultimately of humanity. People who are passive are ideal voters to a government that wants to stay in power. Having been rendered inert by an education that offers them only "fun", they are in no position to read their culture critically, or to see the difference between a garden that has been imagined from the ground up and one that has been bought from a landscape firm's kit.

My English friends get annoyed at having their country treated like a theme-park, though in fact that is the way

View from Hercules monument down transverse avenue
towards the barn in April

England is advertised by the airlines nowadays. And it's the way many people look at gardens too: something to pass through on a mental travelator. I suppose that's what I don't want either: to be "Canada's Gardenland". Are the natives (or the monkeys) expected to wave? As Flannery O'Connor said about the readers of her short stories, their indifference greatly increases the stridency of her voice.

Having made four more garden areas in 1995, I do not imagine going on making many more gardens, however. What I have now is almost more than I can handle, though there is some consolation that each year one pushes back the wilderness and the weeds a little more. But oh, garden writers are full of finger-wagging about weeds. Vita Sackville-West would not allow a herbaceous border that was not well weeded. Surely one of the advantages of such a border is that it need not be, that the effect of the whole conceals the deficiency of its parts. Well, there will never be enough weeding to satisfy some; somewhere there will be vice in the world. I wish that I could believe that all of those weeding grannies did it all themselves, or had a patch larger than a dining table.

As I write this, I glance at a note from my dear friend Maureen about what she misses in what I have written so far: "something about the garden-landscape as a way of reflecting on knowledge or ways of knowing . . . about the way that ideas are more than things that happen in our heads. The garden as a way of asking questions, perhaps, and a response to the fullness of being alive as a human creature."

Well, yes, these are the things that one can rarely articulate for oneself. You see what you are doing, and have done, reflected in the faces and voices of those who look back at you, and so you begin to understand a little the text that you are writing, the text I have written into this landscape . . . and out of it. Part of what you understand is what I have called "rival knowledge", the things that a mechanical culture has suppressed.

I have just been reading Oliver Sacks's *A Leg to Stand On*: a powerful book, not just about his recovery to health from a terrifying injury, but about his recovery of himself as a whole being in the process, the intimate relation between the imagination and the physical body. He is not talking mystical hogwash; nor am I. Nor was Wallace Stevens (the vice-president of Hartford Insurance, after all) when he described his response to the figure of the imagination walking by the ocean at Key West. "Among the meaningless plungings of water and the wind", a dead mechanical world, the imagination was "the single artificer of the world in which she sang . . . and, singing, made".

And so, I sit now on a late summer evening on the new bench by the barn, the Gainsborough bench, under the old maples, almost at the end of a gardening year that began in the snowy lashings of late winter. The new hill-garden by the house, planted with herbs and heathers and recumbent roses and ground covers, begins to come into its own. The new redbud and the *Magnolia stellata* there are flourishing. I can look out my bedroom window and down that hill, reflect on the mess of bramble and wild lilac that was there, and be content. Behind me here, from the beds by the barn, the clovey smell of the early phlox hangs in the air.

I look out across the new memorial to my dear dead Michael, over the wall built by Campbell, into a field of corn that is now more than ten feet tall, and off to a pink sunset that stretches out my cousins' woods in a dark line across the horizon. "*O fortunatos agricolas*" ("O happy countrymen") says the memorial to the young classicist, dead at thirty, who first took a shovel in his hand here to start all this. The rest of Virgil's line, the uninscribed bit in parentheses, is "*si bona norint*" ("if you but knew your happiness"). Perhaps all of this place is contained in that parenthesis.

Maybe this garden, this landscape, is also another sort of parenthesis, a bracketing of something important from the chaos that surrounds it. Perhaps Wallace Stevens was right. Without what he calls "the leaves of sure obliteration" that summer strews on our path, we would achieve nothing, never be moved to do so. But it is a hard lesson, this business of mortality that brings out the full sweet flavour of an evening like this one, with its trace of bitterness.

And what will Stonyground become? Most of all, it will become an enterprise of some kind, and primarily educational: a centre for landscape and garden study, I hope, with seminars and workshops. As I see it now, this will mean taking over the barn completely, eventually: a place for large meetings, and perhaps a permanent library–workroom for projects. Some of this is already beginning to happen in 1995.

The plans for the barn also include two one-storey wings stretching out into the barnyard. One will be designed for the increasing flow of visitors and will have a café and shop. The café will open on to Barn Lawn, so that tea can be had there in the approved manner. The other (matching) wing will be a greenhouse, so that I can both raise more of the plants needed for the gardens and walks and get into selling them. The new cutting and drying bed made this year will be part of that enterprise. My hope is that I can find enterprising younger people to subcontract both these things.

And there will be an arboretum. It is already in the planning stage. Initially my idea was to raise nursery trees to sell, but I think increasingly that the trees should be left to mature and harvest as timber, as was the case in the first garden to be made with trees, Cassiobury, in the 1670s. Extending from the transverse walk to the road, the arboretum will cover about seven acres and form the new approach to the gardens and the walks.

And afterwards? I shall never live to see these trees full-grown, and one of the things that concerns me is the future of all this beyond my time — especially in a country that has no equivalent of the English National Trust, or indeed of the many private trusts and associations that run such gardens in the United States. In odd moments I find myself wondering why we could not have an equivalent of the Landmark Trust in Britain: a private trust, but one in which many landowners participate for a larger good.

Year by year (rodents willing) there will be more and more bulbs in the walks. Year by year the walks themselves will become more manageable. This will probably mean that quite soon the farm vehicles (which now chew them up so badly in the spring and autumn) will have to use the fields themselves. Already Campbell has made a separate entrance for his purposes along the disused railway. There will have to be set-asides in each field too — an extension of what farmers call "headlands" — to spare the walks from muddy destruction.

As ever, there are new beginnings, new starts. Like all of my plans, some of them will come to something, some won't. As I was raking the *potager* this spring I noticed how attractive some of the granite fragments of the glacial till are. And this has led to my commissioning a local silver-smith to create a range of silver pins — The Stones of Stonyground — in which these stones, polished, are set.

Equally, though, a project to make a column out of old agricultural rollers — a column that would have stood at the end of the main avenue — has been frustrated by the two sets of available rollers being different sizes. And so a smaller column is on a medial berm by the spinney. It's not yet finished, I think; it wants something, but I am content now to wait until I know what that is. "To impose is not to discover," Stevens wrote; "to come upon the thing and see it for the first time." What he is talking about is the old meaning of the word *invention*: "*invenio*" ("to come upon"), to come upon what was always there, waiting.

I would like to think that what I am doing is like that: seeing the neglected beauty in the limestone blocks of the neglected stone piles and turning them into steps and walls, for example, or the handsome strength of a barn wall as a garden backdrop. How much more is to be discovered, "invented", I do not know. Already next year's water garden beckons from the old gravel pit . . . and the arboretum . . . and the temple. As I walk into that future, I walk home, secure in the knowledge that the walk is as possible as it is necessary. I hope it is a long walk. Who knows?

Looking towards the barn from the perimeter walk in summer

Appendix

Plant List

achillea *(Achillea)*

aconite *(Eranthis hyemalis)*

ageratum *(Ageratum)*

allium *(Allium)*

artemisia *(Artemisia lactiflora)*

arugula *(Eruca sativa)*

aster *(Aster)*

astilbe *(Astilbe)*

bergenia *(Bergenia)*

bird's-foot trefoil *(Lotus corniculatus)*

bittersweet *(Celastrus)*

black-eyed Susan *(Rudbeckia hirta)*

bladder campion *(Silene cucubalus)*

bloodroot *(Sanguinaria canadensis)*

blue devil *(Echium vulgare)*

blue-eyed grass *(Sisyrinchium montanum)*

bull thistle *(Cirsium vulgare)*

burdock *(Arctium minus)*

buttercup *(Ranunculus)*

Canada thistle *(Cirsium arvense)*

cardinal flower *(Lobelia cardinalis)*

chelone *(Chelone)*

chionodoxa *(Chionodoxa)*

cinquefoil *(Potentilla)*

clematis *(Clematis)*

clover *(Trifolium)*

couch grass *(Agropyron repens)*

cranesbill *(Geranium)*

creeping Charlie *(Glechoma hederacea)*

crocus *(Crocus)*

daffodil *(Narcissus)*

dahlia *(Dahlia)*

dandelion *(Taraxacum officinale)*

day lily *(Hemerocallis)*

delphinium *(Delphinium)*

dianthus *(Dianthus)*

dog rose *(Rosa canina)*
dog-tooth violet *(Erythronium americanum)*
doronicum *(Doronicum cordatum)*
Dutchman's breeches *(Dicentra cucullaria)*
Dutchman's pipe *(Aristolochia durior)*

echinops *(Echinops ritro)*
erigeron *(Erigeron)*
eryngium *(Eryngium)*

fleabane *(Erigeron)*
foxtail lily *(Eremusus)*
fritillaria *(Fritillaria meleagris)*

geum *(Geum)*
goldenrod *(Solidago)*

heather *(Erica)*
helenium *(Helenium)*
helianthus *(Helianthus)*
hellebore *(Helleborus)*
hepatica *(Hepatica)*
hollyhock *(Alcea)*
honeysuckle *(Lonicera)*
horsetail *(Equisetum arvense)*
hosta *(Hosta)*

impatiens *(Impatiens)*
iris *(Iris)*

Jack-in-the-pulpit *(Arisaema triphyllum)*
Jacob's ladder *(Polemoniaceae caeruleum)*
Joe-Pye weed *(Eupatorium purpureum)*

lady's-mantle *(Alchemilla mollis)*
lady's slipper *(Cypripedium)*
lamb's-quarters *(Chenopodium album)*
lamium *(Lamium maculatum)*
lavatera *(Lavatera)*

lemon thyme *(Thymus serphyllum)*
lilac *(Syringa)*
lobelia *(Lobelia)*
Lords and Ladies *(Arum maculatum)*
lupine *(Lupinus)*
lychnis *(Lychnis)*

Madonna lily *(Lilium candidum)*
mallow *(Malva)*
malva *(Malva)*
marigold *(Calendula officinalis)*
marsh mallow *(Hibiscus militaris)*
marsh marigold *(Caltha palustris)*
mayflower *(Maianthemum canadense)*
Michaelmas daisy *(Aster novae-angliae)*
milkweed *(Asclepias)*
money plant *(Lunaria)*
mountain laurel *(Kalmia latifolia)*
mugwort *(Artemisia)*
mullein *(Verbascum thapsus)*

narcissus *(Narcissus)*
nightshade *(Solanum dulcamara)*

Oriental poppy *(Papaver orientale)*
oxeye daisy *(Chrysanthemum leucanthemum)*

peony *(Paeonia)*
petunia *(Petunia)*
phlox *(Phlox)*
pigweed *(Amaranthus retroflexus)*
pink *(Dianthus)*
plantain *(Plantago major)*
porcelaine berry *(Ampelopsis brevipedunculata)*
pulmonaria *(Pulmonaria)*
purslane *(Portulaca oleracea)*

Queen Anne's lace *(Daucus carota)*

red dock *(Rumex acetosella)*
red-hot poker *(Kniphofia uvaria)*
red trillium *(Trillium sessile)*
rheum *(Rhuem palmatum)*
rhododendron *(Rhododendron)*
rose *(Rosa)*
rugosa rose *(Rosa rugosa)*
Russian sunflower *(Helianthus)*

salvia *(Salvia)*
scilla *(Scilla)*
Scotch thistle *(Onopordum acanthium)*
sedum *(Sedum)*
sheep sorrel *(Rumex acetosella)*
shepherd's purse *(Capsella bursa-pastoris)*
showy lady's slipper *(Cypripedium calceolus)*
snowdrop *(Galanthus)*
sow thistle *(Sonchus arvensis)*
spurge *(Euphorbia)*
star magnolia *(Magnolia stellata)*
stonecrop *(Sedum)*
sweet rocket *(Hesperis matronalis)*
sweet William *(Dianthus barbatus)*

tea rose *(Rosa odorata)*
teasel *(Dipsacus laciniatus)*
tiger lily *(Lilium tigrinum)*
toadflax *(Linaria)*
trillium *(Trillium)*
trumpet vine *(Campsis radicans)*
tulip *(Tulipa)*
Turk's-cap lily *(Lilium superbum)*

veronica *(Veronica)*
vinca *(Vinca)*
viper's bugloss *(Echium vulgare)*

wallflower *(Cheiranthus)*
white chelone *(Chelone glabra)*

wild anemone *(Anemone canadensis)*
wild clematis *(Clematis virginiana)*
wild ginger *(Asarum canadense)*
wild leek *(Allium tricoccum)*
wisteria *(Wisteria)*

yellow flag *(Iris pseudacorus)*
yellow loosestrife *(Lysimachia punctata)*

TREES

alder *(Alnus)*
apple *(Malnus)*

basswood *(Tilia americana)*
beech *(Fagus americana)*
black walnut *(Juglans nigra)*
blue beech *(Carpinus caroliniana)*

cedar *(Thuja)*
cypress *(Cupressus sempervirens)*

eastern white cedar *(Thuja occidentalis)*
elm *(Ulmus)*

hawthorn *(Crataegus)*
hop-hornbeam *(Ostrya virginiana)*

larch *(Larix)*
littleleaf linden *(Tilia cordata)*

magnolia *(Magnolia)*
Manitoba maple *(Acer negundo)*
maple *(Acer)*
mountain-ash *(Sorbus)*
Norway spruce *(Picea abies)*

poplar *(Populus)*
purple beech *(Fagus riversii)*

redbud *(Cercis canadensis)*

spruce *(Picea)*

tamarack *(Larix laricina)*
tulip-tree *(Liriodendron tulipifera)*

walnut *(Juglans)*
weeping willow *(Salix babylonica)*
white pine *(Pinus strobus)*
wild apple *(Malus sylvestris)*
wild cherry *(Prunus)*

ACKNOWLEDGEMENTS

Elizabeth Bishop, "Sestina," *The Complete Poems*, New York: Farrar, Straus & Giroux, 1969.

S.T. Coleridge, "This Lime-Tree Bower My Prison," *Selected Poetry and Prose*, ed. Stephen Potter, London: The Nonesuch Press, 1962.

John Clare, "The Flitting," *Selected Poetry*, ed. G. Summerfield, London: Penguin, 1990.

George Herbert, "The Forerunners," *The Works of George Herbert*, ed. F.E. Hutchinson, Oxford: Clarendon Press, 1945.

Gerard Manley Hopkins, "Spring and Fall," *The Poems of Gerard Manley Hopkins*, ed, W.H. Gardner & N.H. Mackenzie, Oxford: Oxford University Press, 1970.

Molly Keane, *Full House*, London: Collins, 1935.

John Milton, "Paradise Lost," *Complete Poems and Major Prose*, ed. M.Y. Hughes, New York: Odyssey Press, 1957.

Lorine Niedecker, "Lake Superior," *Collected Poems 1936-1968*, London: Fulcrum Press, 1970.

Wallace Stevens, "Credences of Summer," *The Palm at the End of the Mind*, New York: Knopf, 1971.

Tom Stoppard, *Arcadia*, London: Faber & Faber, 1993.

Alfred Lord Tennyson, "Ulysses," *The Poems of Tennyson*, ed. Christopher Ricks, London: Longmans, 1969.

Walt Whitman, "When Lilac Last," *Complete Poetry and Selected Prose*, ed. James E. Miller, Boston: Houghton Mifflin, Riverside Editions, 1959.

W.B. Yeats, "Ancestral Houses," *Collected Poems*, 2d ed., London: Macmillan, 1967.